Acknowledgement of Country

We acknowledge the traditional custodians of the lands on which we work and on which this book was produced, and pay our respects to elders past, present and emerging. We recognise that sovereignty was never ceded. Always was always will be. Aboriginal land.

We embrace the principle of 'First Nations First': re-centring Australian history with Indigenous histories. We recognise that Australia's migration history began, and continues, on stolen land that has not been ceded; and that it is untenable to talk about race in Australia without situating it in the histories of dispossession and colonisation of Australia's First Peoples.

PRAISE FOR *AFTER AUSTRALIA*

'*After Australia* offers a glimpse of a national literature that is sharp, lyrical, exciting and uncompromising.'
Maxine Beneba Clarke, *The Age/Sydney Morning Herald*

'When creatives abandon their designated cultural silos to work together on a project, something magical and transformative happens to the Australian literary voice … [*After Australia*'s] breadth and experimentalism mean there should be a pristine copy for the bookshelf and another dog-eared one for your handbag. Each story demands a revisit.' *The Big Issue*

'There is much in this book to fascinate, inspire and provoke.'
Kill Your Darlings

'How the past and present affect or compromise the future is explored here in provocative and sometimes surprising ways.'
The Saturday Paper

'This book challenges and enthralls in equal measure. It is dynamite!' Christos Tsiolkas

Affirm press
books that leave an impression

Published by Affirm Press in 2022
Boon Wurrung Country
28 Thistlethwaite Street,
South Melbourne, VIC 3205
affirmpress.com.au
10 9 8 7 6 5 4 3 2 1

Image of Edward Thomas Te Whiu, page 107: New Zealand Police Files
Image of Mt Eden Prison, page 120: Auckland Libraries Heritage Collection

Gr8ful by Shankari Chandran is an edited extract from *Chai Time at Cinnamon Gardens*, published with permission from Ultimo Press

NATIONAL LIBRARY OF AUSTRALIA
A catalogue record for this book is available from the National Library of Australia

Title: Another Australia / Winnie Dunn, editor.
ISBN: 9781922711687 (paperback)

Cover design by Josh Durham, Design by Committee
Typeset in 11.5pt/19.5pt Minion Pro by J&M Typesetting
Proudly printed in Australia by McPherson's Printing Group

FSC www.fsc.org
MIX
Paper from responsible sources
FSC® C001695

ANOTHER AUSTRALIA

Edited by Winnie Dunn

Diversity Arts Australia
Affirm press
sweatshop.

Tuʻu pē lā mo e poupou

Ensure you are prepared for any eventuality

— Tongan Proverb

CONTENTS

YILAALU

Prologue

Nardi Simpson

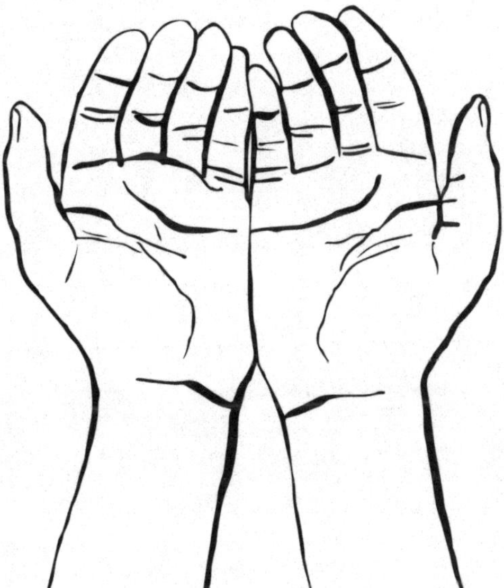

wuuna ngay birralii
wuuna nguungu birralii
wuuna nguungu birralii
wuuna milan-ngu birralii
ganungu wuuna birralii

wuu-na

with Tracey Cameron

dhuyu gaymalaanha dhaymaaya
burrulnha
giirr nhama dhuyugu wambalaanha wirringaa, mari bawaga
nguungunda yanaawaanha ganunga murrilaga yarralga,
yurruli
Nguu ganunga dhirranbalaanha, garriya ganunga.
wanggamalanha ganunga giinbali ghundiga, dhiyaangu
yanawaanha-bula ngaya, ngadaa-bala mubal dhuyugu. waal
gaburranda. waal ngaya wamba!
dhiirralgu ngaya yanawaanha

warrangal nha. giirr nhama gaay, bigan, burrulmaatha
gundidhi nha nganunda yanawaanha
yanawaanha ngaya, mubal dhuyugu ngadaa buudhaaga.
Yaama, ngali guwaalaylanha, ngarriya ngali
milan.
guwiinbaa.
gaba.
ngarrilanha nguungunda waaraalgiirr ngaya
wamba, bayangurr
dhural nganundi biyuurralanha
bundaagilanha ngaya, bina, mil muwilanha gugirriidhalibaa,
yirrgayn
ngarraldanha ngay dhiirral, winangaylanha
giirr dhirralnha gayliyaay. mulabiyaay nha. buudhaagiirr.
burrulaa ngaya dhiirrali-nginda
ngarugilanha ngali. giirr nhama gali wiibiyaay. gaylamala
ngay yili. gindamaylanha ngaya
waal ngaya ngarraldanha buuyan-nha Burruguuga gaay
garay guwaaldanha garriya guwaaldanha, baluwaa gigilaya,
dhiirralgu winangay,
wirringaa-nha dhuyu-giirr-
dhabiyaan,
warranggal,
bawaga nha ganunga wambalaaya

waal-bala ngaya winangay
dhurraamildanha ngaya gudhuwaylanha yanay wuwilanha
ngaya yaluu
girrigirri ngaya, dhina madhanbaa-baraay miyay ngaya
dhiirral ngay gaba. baluwaal nha nganunda gagil
guwaaldanha
dhiirralu nganunda wuurraaya gaay
gaay nha mulabiyaay
giirr nganunda dhiirralu wuurraaya gaba gaay
gaba winangaylanha
wanagilanha ngali, dhiirralanha-nha ngaya
buwabiila ngaya gaylamanhi yili, manduwi nha yiiy,
yananhi-bula, ngadaa-bala mubal dhuyugu gundhigu
dhiirrali ngay nganunda wuurraaya. giirr gaba ngaya
ngarralanha dhiirralga
yilaa ngaya winangali. dhurrali nha ngaya gayaanga.

Give

A snake wriggles across the ground. Large enough to carry men and women on its back. On him they travel across the escarpment, over sandstone, through towering forests. He sheds them and they land. They roll from his scales into the places they wish to be. I walk too, under the belly of the snake. Not on top. I'm not silly! I am going to meet my teacher.

She is powerful. Her thoughts, words, actions are boss. She walks from her house to meet me. I walk from mine, under the snake's belly to our meeting place. We say greetings and we sit down. Close. Connected. The way things should always be.

When I am with her I am like a pup at her feet. Silly and young. Sounds tumble from me, I bump into things, my ears and eyes are closed, blurring and unformed. My teacher watches and listens. She is gentle. She is kind. Patient too – Old ways. I have so much to learn.

We drink. The liquid is hot. In my rush to consume I burn my lips. I laugh. I don't realise the burn is creation's warning. It is saying, stop talking, be slow, listen to your teacher, the woman like the great snake – quiet, powerful, who carries others on her back. I don't listen. I wait for the pain to fade and gulp again. Loud, heavy-footed girl that I am. I crash and kick when I should creep and glide.

My dearest teacher. Never has she said a hard word to me. Only beautiful ones. My teacher gives me language. Her words are soft. She shows me good ways with words. And the right ways to hear them. I learn this only when we have parted. After I have burned my lips and bitten her shoes and walked under the snake back to my home.

My teacher gives me things to know but also ways to be. I feel good when I see my teacher. One day I will know how to listen. Then I will do her proud.

* *illustration by baawaa ngay (my younger sister), Lucy Simpson*

A TALE OF TWO COLONIES

Osman Faruqi

In the northern part of the Indian subcontinent there's a region that was once home to one of the oldest cultures in South Asia. It's known as the Indus Valley Civilisation. The Indus Valley Civilisation existed alongside other historical empires in Western Asia and North Africa, including ancient Egypt and Mesopotamia. It was more geographically widespread than either of its contemporaries and technologically advanced. It consisted of hundreds of planned cities made up of brick houses and marvels of ancient engineering, including complex water and drainage systems. Its citizens were renowned for their craftsmanship. Thousands of pieces of their art, including sculptures made of clay and bronze, statues and jewellery, can be found in museums all over the world.

After 2000 years of existence, the Indus Valley Civilisation collapsed. We don't know why, and probably never will, but the best evidence we have suggests climate change, earthquakes, or a combination of the two. But different cultures and communities in the region have flourished for thousands of years thanks to its proximity to one of the world's mightiest rivers, the Indus, and its tributaries. Those five tributaries, the Jhelum, Chenab,

Ravi, Sutlej and Beas rivers, are where the region derives its name. Known in Ancient Greek as Pentapotamía, in Sanskrit as Pañcanada, in Persian as Panjab, it's now known as Punjab. All translate to 'Land of the five rivers'. Punjab's fertility and proximity to a number of powerful empires made it a regular target for conquest and imperial ambition. It was ruled by a succession of different powers including the Greeks, Scythians, Parthians, Huns, Arabs, Mughals, Afghans and Marathis, before eventually being annexed by the British East India Trading Company and subsumed into the British Empire, at the peak of European colonialism.

For the next one hundred years, Punjab remained a contiguous province under British rule. Its diverse population consisted of Hindus, Sikhs, Muslims and Christians, all speaking the same dialect, eating the same food and sharing the same cultural traditions. Religious differences had long played a part in the internal politics of the subcontinent, and they were ruthlessly exploited by the British, who deployed a strategy of divide and conquer in order to keep their colonial subjects fighting amongst themselves, instead of organising amongst each other to resist the rulers.

For generations the British strategy worked but ultimately solidarity always prevails. During World War II, Indians organised themselves into the largest volunteer army the world has ever seen, a force of two-and-a-half million. They fought the Axis powers alongside the Allies across three continents: Asia, Europe and Africa. The war was a galvanising process for the independence movement. Indians from different religious and cultural backgrounds fought alongside each other, on behalf of their British rulers. They played a vital role in helping to defeat the Nazis and the Japanese Empire, and they wanted their reward: freedom. After hundreds of years of agitation, culminating in decades of violent protests, riots and mass civil disruption, the anti-colonial movement finally succeeded in expelling the British Empire and freeing India from imperial rule.

Even though the Indian independence movement only succeeded because it was diverse and pan-religious, centuries of oppression and division had created fear and resentment amongst many. Some Muslims feared that in an independent India they would be marginalised by the country's Hindu majority. They advocated for their own state, a country governed by Muslims for Muslims.

So, in 1947, one of the greatest tragedies in modern history took place: the partition of India along religious lines. Punjab was where the schism was most acutely and violently felt. As one of the most religiously diverse regions in India, its future was hotly contested. It had a slim Muslim majority, which Muslim leaders argued should see it belong to the newly created Muslim-governed dominion of Pakistan. Hindu leaders argued that significant portions of the region had Hindu majorities, who wouldn't be safe in Pakistan. Sikhs were worried they would be caught in the middle.

To resolve the dispute the British sent a lawyer, Cyril Radcliffe, to India to consult and finalise boundary plans. After arriving in India, Radcliffe was given just five weeks to decide how to divide a region that had, more or less, remained a cohesive state since the days of the Indus Valley Civilisation thousands of years before. Radcliffe had never before been to India. In fact, the closest he had ever been to the subcontinent was Paris. Ultimately, he drew a line somewhere along the middle of Punjab, dividing communities, households and families. What followed was one of the largest forced population displacements in human history, along with mass violence. An estimated twenty million people were displaced as Muslims fled India for the newly created country of Pakistan and Hindus fled to India. Up to two million people were killed.

Partition was a horrific and traumatic end to British colonialism on the subcontinent and its ramifications will be felt for generations. Partition is also the reason for my existence. My father's father was a soldier from Uttar Pradesh, in what is now India, who enlisted during World War II hoping to fight. He was still in training when the war ended and so his first deployment ended up being domestic peacekeeping. His unit was given command of a confiscated German half-track and ordered to patrol the streets of Calcutta during the violent sectarian protests that broke out during partition. Like all Muslim soldiers who resided in what had just become India, he was given the option to stay or to migrate to Pakistan – the country that had been created ostensibly for people like him. Without the opportunity to speak to his family and knowing that he might never see them again, he decided that he would accept the offer of a ship to Pakistan and attempt to rebuild his life there. He eventually settled in Punjab.

My mother's grandfather was a pro-independence activist and politician, closely allied to Mohammad Ali Jinnah – Pakistan's founding father. He was an advocate for partition, wanting a homeland for India's Muslim minority and went on to become one of the longest serving speakers in the Punjab legislative assembly. There's a street named after him in Punjab's capital, Lahore, the city where my parents met and where I was born. Like so many millions of others, in so many countries around the world, my very existence is the result of intertwined political and social forces across hundreds of years.

It's easy to think of these things as coincidences – a soldier leaving his family behind to try and make his life in a new country, whose son ends up marrying the granddaughter of a politician that fought to create the country – but framing something as a coincidence absolves those in power of responsibility. All of the consequences of partition, from the violence, the chaos, the death, the millions of refugees, the numerous wars, the ongoing trauma, to the seemingly coincidental stories of love and the creation of new families, are the result of a series of deliberate decisions. Decisions to conquer, to colonise, to rule, to loot, to impoverish, to divide.

My parents' decision to leave one former colony for another is the end result of a series of similar decisions. The relative poverty, economic disadvantage, violence and endemic corruption of former colonies like India and Pakistan are directly related to the industrial-scale theft of wealth carried out by the colonisers. An estimated $60 trillion, in today's terms, was plundered from British India during colonial rule.

It was the wealth of colonies like India that allowed the British to colonise the continent known as Australia.

In 1622, the crew of the *Tryall* became the first British sailors to sight Australia's western coast. The ship was owned by the British East India Company, the corporation that first annexed the Indian subcontinent. The nine merchant ships that made up the bulk of the First Fleet were all either owned by or under lease to the British East India Company. The company was used for decades to ferry convicts to the new colony, and in return was granted a monopoly on all trade in and out of it. When supplies were running short the early colonial leaders in New South Wales turned to British India for rice and wheat, farmed and processed by Indian farmers and shipped on British East India Company vessels.

Numerous colonial settlers moved from India to the new colony in the years after invasion. The wealth of English settlers in India would buy them more land and authority in Australia than it would back in the motherland. One example is that of Sydney Watson, the son of a Scotsman born in Calcutta in 1816. Eighteen years later he arrived in New South Wales. He became a wealthy pastoralist by buying up cheap land from colonial authorities. He named one of his stations, on the border of Queensland and the Northern Territory, 'Punjaub' . The cattle station had five rivers running through it up to the Gulf of Carpentaria. It was Watson's ode to the country of his birth.

Australia's early colonial infrastructure was also deeply reliant on those who had practised the craft on the subcontinent. Judges, administrators and traders moved from India to settle in Australia. Four of New South Wales' s first five governors had all served in India, including Lachlan Macquarie. Macquarie lived in India for over a decade and fought numerous battles against Indian forces, helping conquer the subcontinent for the British. During his time in India, Macquarie bought an Indian slave, George Jarvis. He brought Jarvis with him to Australia. On the trip over, Jarvis was referred to by one of Macquarie's colleagues, the future judge advocate of New South Wales, Ellis Bent, as 'a black Hindu servant of Colonel Macquarie's'. Macquarie is directly responsible for numerous massacres of Indigenous people throughout New South Wales. He also gave explicit instructions to soldiers to fire upon and hang Indigenous people if they resisted his attempts to 'clear the country'. The British explicitly used the wealth, resources and experience they had developed in colonising India to first invade Australia and then commit violent genocide on its Indigenous inhabitants.

In some instances, the role of Britain's Indian subjects was more explicit. Throughout the 1800s there were thousands of Indians in Australia working as cameleers and explorers, including alongside Burke and Wills in their infamous expedition. While colloquially and historically referred to as 'Afghans', most were Muslims drawn from British India, including Punjab. Despite the fact that they were subject to discrimination because of their racial background and appearance, the cameleers were instrumental in the early part of the colonial project. Even though many ended up settling in Indigenous communities and starting families, their overall contribution was to help the colonists map and conquer the rest of the continent on behalf of Britain.

The British never saw India as a continent where they would try to eradicate the local population and populate it with a White majority. But that's exactly how they saw Australia, and they used India, and Indians, to help them do it. Which is precisely why my family's presence, like that of many migrants from former colonies, is not a coincidence. The Australian colonial project was about erasing the original inhabitants, occupying their land and using the wealth generated to build a European outpost in Asia.

Most White Australians are, of course, in denial about this. Bizarrely they seem to think that the relative richness of Australia versus countries like India and Pakistan is the result of hard work, luck or ingenuity, as opposed to a series of specific processes designed precisely to create this situation. And so of course, that kind of deliberate global inequality leads to an influx of migrants from one part of the world (the Global South) to countries that have money and perceived economic opportunity primarily thanks to the violence they committed on Indigenous people, and what they exploited from their former colonies.

This situation causes confusion amongst many post-colonial migrants to Australia. We're here because of how colonialism shaped our home countries, but we're also on the stolen land of those who themselves have been subject to even more violent colonial forces. We aren't White but we occupy a more privileged place in society. We experience racism but we also perpetuate it.

Many of these experiences aren't new. In colonial India lateral violence was common and encouraged by the British. Lighter-skinned Indians from the north discriminated against darker-skinned Indians in the south. Those who were taught English by colonial authorities in turn looked down upon those without that opportunity. Muslims and Hindus discriminated against each other. That's the sad irony of how colonialism has always, and will always, play out.

Colonial subjects are often manipulated into thinking that by acquiescing to the demands of those in power, they might themselves be rewarded with power of their own. Ultimately, it's a futile endeavour.

White colonists have made it clear time and time again, on continent after continent, that it doesn't matter how close to power you think you're getting or how useful you might have been to the colonial project. When you stop being useful or become a threat, you'll be discarded.

The *Immigration Restriction Act*, which formed the foundational pillar of the White Australia policy, is probably the best-known example of this truism. It wasn't just Indian and Afghan cameleers who were impacted, but Chinese, Japanese and Pasifika workers who had laboured to build the colony for White colonists and were deported and banned from re-entering once Australia had federated. Even those who weren't deported suffered legal discrimination that spoke to how White Australians perceived all those who weren't White.

In 1902, Australia's federal parliament passed the *Commonwealth Franchise Act*. To most people it's known as the law that gave women the right to vote and stand for parliament, making Australia the first democracy in the world to do so. What's less well known is that while the Act enfranchised women for the first time at a federal level, it also stripped the franchise from virtually all non-Whites in Australia. While most Australian parliaments had accepted the need to extend voting rights to women, there was concern that the political power of working White men would be diluted. So the compromise was to strip voting rights from non-Whites.

The Senate debate at the time is depressingly clear as to what was motivating Australia's first politicians. Senator James Styles, a Protectionist Party representative from Victoria, said: 'It is an inconsistency that a woman should not have a vote, although she may employ a large number of people, and have a considerable stake in the country, whilst a Chinese gardener has the franchise … The Chinaman does not spend more than a few shillings a year on his clothing, and – if I may use such an expression – will live upon a bag of rice and the smell of an oil rag for six months.' Queensland Labor Senator Thomas Glassey was even explicit about his reason for wanting to prevent non-Whites from voting. 'It is all very well for honourable senators to be benevolently inclined towards Aboriginals and coloured aliens,' he argued. 'But that policy means letting loose a large number of persons who will be able to affect our elections in Queensland in a manner that will be detrimental to the interests of that State and of the whole Commonwealth.' Another Labor Senator from Western Australia even spelled out at the electoral maths: 'We have to remember that there are somewhere about 80,000 of the coloured races in Australia apart from Aborigines. It is said that there are 200,000 Aborigines in Australia.' And so, just like with the *Immigration Restriction Act* passed a year before, Australia's colonial leaders decided that their power was being threatened by those who had helped them amass it, and they neutered them. The Australian Senate amended the bill to read, 'No aboriginal native of Australia, Asia, Africa, or the islands of the Pacific, or persons of the half-blood shall be entitled to have his name placed on an electoral roll [unless otherwise enfranchised by the state they reside in].' The House of Representatives agreed with the amendment, with one small change – it removed the reference to 'half-blood'.

And so, thirty-two years after Black men in the United States were granted the right to vote (although in practice this was severely curtailed), Australia removed it for all non-Whites. It's an extraordinary story, not just because it further highlights how racist Australia's political history has been, but because of the simplistic and consistent manner in which people from all non-White backgrounds were treated in this context. The vast majority of the world's population, from Africa, to China, to Japan, to India, to the Pacific Islands, to Indigenous people in Australia, were lumped together in one sentence: 'Aboriginal natives of Australia, Asia, Africa, or the islands of the Pacific.' It was an explicit reminder that while colonialism might seek to elevate one race or minority over another, it only does so in order to further itself, and it ultimately seeks to subjugate everyone.

Of course, on a day-to-day basis the treatment of Indigenous people was markedly more discriminatory and violent than that of Chinese, Japanese and Indian migrants (as it continues to be). But the fact that White politicians felt they were in opposition to all non-Whites when passing this bill is significant.

Siva Singh, like me, was born in Punjab. Like me, he

moved to Australia. But unlike me, he arrived here before Australia existed, prior to Federation, in 1897. He settled in north-eastern Victoria and became a hawker. According to records from the time, he was well known to the local community and easily identifiable by his pink turban. He was also part of one of the most important, and least well-known, civil rights campaigns in Australia. Singh was not impressed by the *Commonwealth Franchise Act*. He felt as though he had contributed to the country, paid taxes, played by the rules, and was being rewarded by being disenfranchised. He took the matter to court, lost, appealed all the way through to the High Court and lost again. Even though his legal challenges failed, Singh sparked a conversation about the rights of Indians in Australia. The campaign he started gained momentum during World War I when Australian and Indian troops fought alongside each other in Gallipoli. *The Woman Voter*, a monthly magazine in favour of women's suffrage, editorialised in favour of Singh: 'If Indians are our "brothers" when it comes to a question of helping us kill our "enemies", they must also be regarded as our brothers in Australian citizenship.'

In 1925, the law was eventually amended again to allow Australians of Indian descent to vote. Even though there was a domestic push for such a change, spurred on by Singh's case, it was ultimately pressure from Britain that pushed Australia's politicians to act. A key turning point was the Amritsar massacre in Punjab in 1919. A large crowd mobilised to protest the arrest of a number of key independence leaders. British soldiers fired on the crowd, killing over a thousand innocent civilians. The violent response sparked protests across the country. Punjab was placed under martial law and several high-profile independence activists, including my mother's grandfather, were placed under house arrest. Two years later, at the Imperial Conference, British government officials pleaded with Australia to grant Indians in the country more civil rights. Indian officials were pressuring Australia and South Africa for equal treatment for Indian nationals across the Commonwealth. Britain was also under pressure due to the rising tide of pro-independence sentiment in India. Four years later parliament acquiesced, with those in favour of the amendment arguing that Australia needed to do its bit to quell independence sentiment in Punjab and across India. They also reassured politicians hesitant about the change that thanks to the success of the *Immigration Restriction Act*, there were only around 2000 Indians still in Australia, so the rights being afforded to Indian Australians were more symbolic than tangible.

It wasn't for another thirty-seven years that the provision first inserted in 1902 was completely repealed, finally removing race-related legal voting barriers (though in practice they still exist) at a federal level. One of the most vocal proponents at the time was Labor's Gough Whitlam. In 1961, he argued that an Aboriginal person was denied the vote '... not because he is in any way inferior to his fellow citizens, but because he is an Aboriginal'. Thirteen years later, as prime minister, Whitlam would be captured in one of the most iconic photos in Australian history, pouring sand into the hand of land rights activist Vincent Lingiari. The picture was taken by Mervyn Bishop, the first Indigenous person to work on a metropolitan daily newspaper. I met Merv at the funeral of a family friend in central-west New South Wales a few years ago. He caught my eye, and came up to me. 'Fancy running into another curry-muncher out here!' he said to me. Before I had a chance to reply he introduced himself. 'My name's Merv, and my grandfather was Punjabi. Where are you from?'

We were both extremely excited to meet a fellow Punjabi and I was particularly excited to discover that I had something in common with one of Australia's greatest news photographers. He told me a bit about his family and how his grandfather settled with local Indigenous families because they welcomed him more warmly than White Australians did. He told me about how when he was growing up he sometimes wasn't sure how he fit in, because not many people where he was from had mixed Punjabi and Indigenous heritage. He told me he wished he knew more about where his grandfather was from in Punjab, and what brought him to Australia.

It was Merv's story that made me first really think about the relationship between those two colonies, the similarities and the differences. It made me think about a time before colonisation, before the political, social and economic forces that ripped apart communities, cultures and language groups existed. Before some marginalised groups felt like they had to side with the oppressor instead of others who were marginalised. It made me think about what kind of world we would be living in if solidarity always won out, if we had been able to resist better, harder, and if we had chosen the right sides. It made me think about me, and my place in this colony, where I belong, where I should be, and what I should be doing.

But most significantly, it helped me realise that nothing is static, immovable or unchangeable. What we call Australia hasn't always been like this. It doesn't need to be like this. A series of explicit decisions made by a particular set of people made it like this. Other decisions, overwhelmingly taken by those whose land was stolen, have already helped unmake it. It can, and will, be unmade.

BAD TRANSPLANT

Amani Haydar

1

Almost one million people left Lebanon during the civil war. Mariam told herself she was leaving for love, not fear, though her plane flew out of Beirut the day after Prime Minister Karami's helicopter came down. Sitting in her narrow seat, she was two types of nervous. First, she was nervous about being so far from the ground in this big bullet. Every time it jolted, she pictured its twisted metal casing against some cliff face or strewn through a desert. People and luggage like confetti. Second, she was nervous about meeting *him*. Qasim. The man from the little photo her aunt Khadija had placed in her hand six months earlier. It had been taken in her mother's village, before Qasim left for Australia, then passed from one hand to the next in search of its nasib until it found her palm. 'He's a distant relative. Lives in Australia. Ma helou?' her aunt said as she handed it to her. 'I go back to Australia in a few weeks, you can travel with me.' Mariam tilted her head to one side without answering. She lifted the small grey photo towards her nose, examining Qasim's high cheekbones and plump bottom lip. Yes, he was handsome. She liked this face. She liked the way he gazed from the smooth paper towards a nondescript and distant point. She imagined that the distant point must have been Australia and she longed to gaze at it too.

2

Now that she was on the plane, bridal gifts of gold and lingerie from Damascus packed in a suitcase, a sneaky inner voice hissed, 'What if he's *awful*?' Every time this voice teased, the well-mannered and faithful part of her answered, 'He is a nice man from a nice family and I will love him. There isn't a problem between man and wife that can't be fixed with a bit of sabr and a bit of imaan.'

To one side sat Aunt Khadija who was chubby and smelled of musk. On the other side sat Qasim's older brother, Yusuf, who was the last of his siblings to migrate to Australia. He'd timed his flight so that he could accompany Mariam and Aunt Khadija. So far, he'd been insufferable. After meals, he'd let out a loud burp then shut his eyes and sleep with his arms crossed, whistling through his nose hairs. His knees filled the already cramped space between rows and Mariam had to squeeze past him whenever she needed to get to the bathroom. He apologised – 'Sorry ya-akhti!' – each time her knees bumped his but never once offered to get up and move into the aisle so that she could pass with ease.

Qasim didn't seem anything like Yusuf; she'd been reassured of his hygiene, wit and good manners. But the voice persisted anyway: 'What if he's *awful*?' She remembered saying these exact words to her childhood friend May, who'd married a year ago and was living in Melbourne with her husband who was said to be very good-looking and highly educated. May had sent Mariam a photo of herself in a white dress and fascinator, with the words 'ktiir helwi Australia' scrawled on the back in blue biro. Mariam wondered how far Sydney was from Melbourne and whether Qasim might know May's husband.

Relying on the few words that had come from May and the descriptions shared by village elders bragging about the jobs and homes their sons had secured abroad, Mariam had conjured an Australia to daydream about as she counted down the days to her flight: an island with big houses arranged in neat rows around a sparkling harbour. She embellished this image with visions of herself in good dresses, a handsome Qasim and their very own car. Electricity that never ran out. No politicians falling out of skies.

3

Once they had landed and their papers and bags had been checked, Mariam walked tepidly over the speckled linoleum floor of the airport. As her luggage rolled beside her, she searched faces in the crowd for Qasim. The flight had been so dominated by Lebanese migrants, and the terminal so full of eager Lebanese families, that at first she forgot that she was in a new country.

When she spotted Qasim, he was standing on his toes, scanning the crowd. He was wearing acid-wash jeans and a leather jacket. He was as handsome as the photo she'd been given albeit slightly thinner than she'd imagined. Mariam's heart rushed, *da-dom da-dom*, until she could hear it in her ears. She jostled past strangers towards Qasim, bags swinging side to side with each step. Yusuf and Aunt Khadija walked a metre or two behind her. She smiled at Qasim as they made eye contact. Qasim waved and rushed towards her and then right past her into the arms of Yusuf. They kissed each other's cheeks, patted each other's backs and Qasim began to take Yusuf's bags from him. As Mariam watched Qasim rub his forehead against Yusuf's, it occurred to her all at once that she was still a stranger to these people and this place.

Aunt Khadija was to chaperone Mariam until she and Qasim had signed their marriage contract before the Sheikh. Aunt Khadija caught up and put a hand on Mariam's shoulder and said, 'Don't worry, you will get used to each other.' She gave Mariam's shoulder a squeeze. 'Bas el-dam bi-henn.' Blood longs for blood.

4

Eight days later, Mariam and Qasim signed their marriage paperwork in Aunt Khadija's backyard with the Sheikh and about twenty relatives. Aunt Khadija got some women to help her prepare a big lunch – everything from mansaf to prawn cocktails. Mariam wore a candy-pink satin dress with matching elbow-length gloves and, for the first time ever, lipstick. Qasim wore a black tuxedo with a pink cummerbund.

Afterwards, a taxi dropped Mariam and Qasim off at their new home. Their apartment was above a row of shops on Beamish Street in Campsie. Mariam followed Qasim through a small square foyer and up a tight staircase, white pumps clip-clopping over loose tiles. She felt a squeeze in her chest as she stepped onto the landing. The front door to the apartment was pale blue except for the number, which looked like it had been drawn on with a black marker. Qasim kissed Mariam on the forehead and turned the key. 'I'm really excited to have you here.' He smiled. She smiled back, even though the squeeze in her chest was now a lump in her throat.

The door swung open and Mariam looked around. The apartment was so small she could see the lounge room, the kitchen, a balcony and the end of a corridor from where she stood. The furniture was dated and mismatched and the only decorative item in the room was a large ceramic rooster with beady eyes on a small coffee table. A square television sat in a TV unit against one of the walls opposite a brown striped couch with a photo of Qasim's late father hanging above it. The kitchen had pale-pink lino floors and beige cabinets – two of which Mariam would find had broken hinges.

When they lay in bed that night, she noticed that the ceiling rose around the pendant light in her bedroom was chipped and eroded so that the floral motifs looked like horned demons in the dark.

5

Blood longs for blood but Aunt Khadija was the only blood Mariam had in Sydney. She came to visit after Mariam's first few nights with Qasim. She brought a white marble-looking statue of a curvy woman draped in a translucent sheet, which Mariam found embarrassing to look at. Mariam said, 'Thank you, you shouldn't have troubled yourself,' and put the woman down next to the rooster. When Aunt Khadija left, Mariam moved both figurines into the bottom shelf of the TV unit.

Mariam settled into her wedded routine. Her husband snored beside her until 4am when his alarm would ring for work. He'd tap her on the shoulder, which was his way of demanding breakfast and a zawedi. She'd say, 'Of course, habibi,' as she rose and shuffled to the kitchen. When Qasim was gone, she'd watch television while cooking and cleaning. Slowly, she began to pick up some English from the shows she watched. The Australia on the television was more like the one she'd imagined before arriving in her sweaty apartment with Beamish Street buzzing beneath it. She tried to make herself believe that this was her Australia too, but she struggled to convince Qasim that they should go anywhere on the weekends. He only wanted to visit Yusuf and a couple of men from work. They languished in apartments as hideous as hers but seemed completely oblivious to it.

6

What Qasim and the Beamish Street apartment lacked in warmth, Mariam fulfilled in daydreams. She had always been good at visualising things. She picked up the habit as a child, as a way of entertaining herself, and honed the skill during the Israeli invasion in 1982, while she and her family were bunkered at a neighbour's house. An older cousin, Amal, had instructed the children to close their eyes whenever the sounds of war grew too frightening. 'T'khayalo halkon bi wadi!', and, as instructed, Mariam would imagine herself in a serene valley. When the food was scarce and all they had for dinner were mushy boiled potatoes to spread on bread, Amal said, 'Imagine yourselves eating lamb and rice and nuts and sweets.' Mariam could conjure a spread so vivid she could smell it.

None of the children could remember how many days they'd been down there and none of them ever talked about the time they'd spent hiding. After the war, the little boys left the bunker to play battle on the dirt roads and the girls sat under trees dreaming things up. Mariam learned she could step into rooms within herself that felt more real than the spaces she physically inhabited. She could reconfigure people, talk to them, correct them. She could escape pain and conflict, simulate pleasure and adventure. With this skill she was able to keep herself happy on her Island for the first year of her marriage.

7

When Mariam fell pregnant, Qasim took her to a male doctor. He was a senior Arab man with a moustache that was tobacco-yellow above the upper lip. His name was Dr Ismail and his office smelled like window cleaner. He said, 'Hmm,' as he touched the top of her belly and then 'Ah-ha!' as he touched the lower parts of her abdomen. Then Dr Ismail sent her behind a curtain for a pelvic exam. She wasn't sure why and had no idea what to expect. The doctor spoke through the curtain to Qasim. They were discussing politics. Mariam lay back, squeezed her eyes shut and tried to go to her Island. She almost jumped when she felt the cold metal of the speculum. *Island, Island, Island.* She grimaced through the discomfort until Dr Ismail finally pulled the metal device away. She waited for him to disappear behind the curtain before she moved.

Dr Ismail spoke only to Qasim when he said everything was fine and that the pregnancy was progressing well. Mariam's muscles softened at these words but she left Dr Ismail's rooms a little dazed and confused.

'You weren't embarrassed at all in there,' jibed Qasim as they got into their old Datsun. His thick eyebrows curled into a frown and his eyes dug into hers as he lit a cigarette.

'What does that mean?' replied Mariam defensively as she buckled her seatbelt.

'You know what I mean,' Qasim snapped, before starting the car and taking off with a jerk of the steering wheel.

Mariam froze. She had no idea how to respond to what Qasim was saying. She wasn't even sure what he was implying. They drove home in silence and when they got to their apartment, she found an excuse to go to bed. She lay under the demons with her eyes closed, doing her best to resurrect Qasim from the photo, trying her hardest to revive the Australia she'd pursued.

8

As her body grew big and unruly, Mariam felt the Beamish Street apartment shrink even smaller. She was a planet in an ever-tightening orbit. At least Qasim never brought up the gynaecologist again. In fact, when Mariam gave birth to a healthy baby boy in a pool of blood, Qasim jumped for joy and kissed her on the forehead just like he used to. He named the boy Zain. Mariam settled into a new routine with Zain. Most days, she'd get the cleaning done in the morning while he was calm. Then she'd put him in the pram for a wander down Beamish Street or catch the bus to a Lebanese grocer called Al-Balad a few streets away where they used the allowance Qasim left her each day to buy things for dinner. She tried to be clever with this spending to show Qasim how responsible she was but also because he wasn't earning enough for her to indulge in anything other than what was necessary.

Mariam and Zain were on their way home from Al-Balad one day when her pram hit a bump in the pavement and lost a wheel. The wheel popped right off the axle and careened down a driveway into the middle of the road where it fell to a stop. Mariam didn't dare retrieve it. There was no way she could leave Zain unsecured on the side of the road, nor would she risk carrying him into the middle of the street to get the wheel.

Even if she were able to get it, it was unlikely she'd be able to fix the pram. 'Ya Allah,' she sighed.

At first, Mariam tried pushing Zain towards the bus stop on the three remaining wheels but the load was awkward and unsteady, weighed down on one side by a bag of groceries. Mariam stopped, took Zain out and carried him on her hip while dragging the broken pram and groceries along with her. This didn't work either. She was soon out of breath and realised she had already missed the bus. Mariam left the pram on the side of the road and accepted that she'd have to walk the remainder of the way. Qasim would probably beat her home and worry but there was no other way about it.

By the time she got home, her arms were sore and she could smell the sweat through her jumper. Her breasts ached because she was late for Zain's afternoon feed. She opened the door and glanced around for Qasim. He was on the balcony with his back to her. She dropped onto the couch and began unfastening her bra to feed Zain. She called out to Qasim, 'I'm sorry we're so late. I'm sure you're hungry.' He slowly put out his cigarette in a glass ashtray, turned towards her and slid the screen door wide open so that it crashed against the frame.

'Where the bloody hell were you?' he yelled, specks of saliva projecting from his bottom lip. Mariam couldn't help but gasp and clasp a hand over her mouth. Startled, Zain released his latch and began to wail.

'Shhhhh,' Mariam hushed to settle the baby as Qasim stood looking down at them.

'Don't bother with dinner. I'm going straight to bed,' he snarled, spittle glazing his plump bottom lip. Then he stormed down the corridor and out of view.

After putting Zain to sleep, Mariam spent the evening by herself but not quite alone. She spent it with the Qasim from the black-and-white photo. She made him take her to the harbour where they took photos of the bridge. 'I'll send them back to my family,' she whispered, reaching for his translucent body. Having completely forgotten her surroundings, she'd spoken the words out loud.

9

In another Australia, Mariam might have asked for help. On a couple of occasions, she almost did. The first time she almost said something to a bank teller. She'd gone into the bank after the birth of her second child to open a savings account for money she'd received in an envelope from May. The teller had a voluminous blonde bob and a golden clover hung around her neck. She was pushy in a way that reminded Mariam of her mother. 'Do you have your ID with you?'

'Um, my husband has that and I don't want to —' Mariam had started answering.

The restless teller interrupted: 'Now, darl, I want you to go home and tell hubby that you need those documents in order to open your account.' Mariam didn't want to explain. Why couldn't she just put the money into an account? The teller was frowning at her and Mariam felt like she was about to be ejected from the building. 'Now I have to serve the lady behind you. I'll see you when you get back,' the teller insisted. Mariam didn't go back and she didn't ask her husband for the documents. Instead, she slipped the notes into the pocket of one of her old coats.

The second time, she tried to tell Aunt Khadija but struggled to explain what it was about Qasim that worried her.

'Did he hit you?' Aunt Khadija asked in a hushed and serious tone.

'No! Nothing like that!' Mariam quickly clarified.

Aunt Khadija laughed. 'Oh good. I can tolerate men as long as they don't do that!'

Mariam decided to let it go. How could she explain that she was in love with a life that existed only in her mind?

Aunt Khadija had died before Mariam could figure out what she wanted to say, killed in cold blood during an Israeli bombing while on holiday in Lebanon. Mariam and Qasim watched a news story about it when it happened. They were living in Bankstown by that point – in an affordable-housing apartment that had been newly built but already had cracks in the render and drainage problems whenever it rained too hard.

The story about Australian citizens dying in the bombing had aired right after a story about an offensive ad Tourism Australia had made. It featured a skinny blonde lady walking on a beach and saying, 'So where the bloody hell are you?'

Qasim got up and lit a cigarette. He grumbled, 'Down the toilet, that's where. And nobody givin' a shit.' Then he left the room.

Whenever Mariam had tried to tell on Qasim or ask for advice, she felt guilty. She thought of Qasim in the photo. Qasim stepping out of the photo. Qasim holding her hand. Qasim on her Island. Qasim taking her to the beach where they would stroll up and down talking about nothing like they were in *Home and Away.* Qasim taking her to see the New Year's Eve fireworks at the harbour. Driving into the sunset with Qasim. Bounding into the sun with Qasim on the back of a kangaroo. Falling into a billabong with Qasim, bodies gliding towards one another in the cool water.

10

All her husband had ever done was work and lie to himself. Now he was dying. They'd lived their lives together and yet the best parts of him had remained forever closed to her. Mariam had spent thirty years trying not to hate or blame him but she resented that they'd never moved forward. Home was now a fibro house in the middle of a street of new builds. It belonged to the government and that meant she couldn't make any improvements on the fibro shack without involving Public Housing, not that she could afford them herself. From Campsie to Bankstown to Villawood, their lives had been pushed further and further out, like the city was ejecting them. A bad transplant. Qasim was waiting for a transplant. His kidneys were sick. He spent their days between the dialysis machine and the front porch where he smoked away any good the treatment was doing. Mariam resented that Qasim had gone and aged and made himself unwell. But she'd never mustered the courage to tell him that. She managed him now, putting food before him and saying the right things like, 'Allah yehfazak!' The words formed in her mouth but not in her heart. Somewhere along the way, the other Qasim and the other Australia that had kept her moving forward had slipped from reach.

A few streets away was the detention centre. Every now and then, a mysterious loud horn went off there. She assumed it signalled some emergency. The place reminded her of that line in the *Willy Wonka and the Chocolate Factory* movie that her kids made her watch: 'Nobody ever goes in, and nobody ever comes out!' Of course, people did go in. Twice in the last four years her son Zain had said, 'Did you see the news? Someone died there last night.'

It had been 215 days since the mouldy cornices had fallen from the bathroom ceiling. Mariam had just finished cleaning the floors when it happened, and it had sent debris all over the old beige tiles that she'd already worked so hard to make decent. 'This bloody house,' she'd grumbled under her breath. It had taken at least five calls to get the Public Housing people to come out to fix them.

She took a Valium as the handymen got to work, rested her head back on the sofa and started falling asleep to the sound of chisel and grinder cutting into plaster, hammer and nail in gyprock. She squeezed her eyes but it had gotten harder and harder to conjure her Island. Instead, a tall grey gum tree flickered. Six crows sat on a powerline. A storm cloud rolled over. A flash of lightening burnt the retina. A stretch of red sand bled into view and turned into burnt bush. A voice, disembodied, boomed, 'Where the bloody hell are you?'

COI BÓI

Shirley Le

Fortune-telling isn't an ethnic thing, it's a dumbass thing. When I was eleven, my mum decided to visit a thầy bói. Through her professional network, the Australia Post sorting facility in Clyde, she had heard about a legendary mystic who could predict the future with eerie accuracy. At home, chewing through rounds of bitter melon stuffed with minced pork, Mum relayed to us what Chú Tùng, her supervisor at work, had told the ladies of Mail Room One earlier that day.

As she spoke, Mum's pale fingers fiddled with the jade Buddha pendant hanging from the delicate gold chain around her neck. She wore that necklace everywhere, except when she showered. I was not allowed to touch it because I had a track record of either losing or breaking stuff. 'Why do I waste money buying things for such a clumsy little girl?' Mum would scold. I was the Gollum to her precious belongings. One day, when water gushed from the showerhead, I'd prised open the black velvet jewellery box on her bedside table like it was the shell of an oyster and scooped out the necklace with the cartoonish glee of the Hamburglar. Cupped in both hands, the stone felt heavy and cool against my skin. I watched white clouds tumbling from the tiny Buddha's smiling face to his shoulders and melting against the lush green earth at the foot of his robes. It seemed odd that such a serene being hung from the neck of the most neurotic person on the planet. The squeak of the shower tap signalled that it was time to put the necklace back.

Now, as Mum talked about the mystic, she twirled the jade Buddha between her fingertips. It was obvious from the way Dad did not look up from his rice that she needed some divine intervention. 'Five years ago, Chú Tùng decided to visit a mystic. She shuffled some cards and informed him that during a palindromic year, he could expect to experience a significant loss followed by a significant gain.' Mum paused and sliced the edge of her metal spoon through some steamed pork. She chewed, letting what she had just told us marinate in the air.

I did the maths in my head. The last palindromic year was three years ago: 2002. That's the year Chú Tùng's wife filed for divorce and also the year he became supervisor of Mail Room One. I remembered hearing Mum gossiping about it to her friends while standing at the counter at Thanh's Bánh Mì in Bankstown, the main selling point of which was that it hadn't been slapped with a penalty notice from the New South Wales Food Authority yet. While waiting for my pork roll with no chilli and extra pâté, I heard about Chú Tùng's wife claiming to have found true love with Harold Hartog, an old White real estate agent who lurked near the nail salon in Bass Hill where she worked. Apparently, the news hit Chú Tùng worse than the two major injuries of his life: '74, when Viet Cong shrapnel shredded his butt, leaving him with an eternal two-point-five-second gap between each footstep, and '91, when a malfunky forklift in a Woolies warehouse unloaded a box of eggs onto his left shoulder.

I wasn't allowed to watch a lot of TV so I was very entertained by the gossip. One day, I'd be the Viet Perez Hilton reporting on the community. I'd already heard about that forklift injury straight from the compo claimant's mouth. Dad snuck out to a drinking party one evening when Mum was on shift at the Post and brought me along. Chú Tùng was there, faded on Hennessy and delivering a monologue about his life to anyone who would listen. From what I understood of his rant, it wasn't the box landing on his shoulder that caused the damage, but a tiny fragment of eggshell that had lodged in his left eyeball, millimetres from blinding him and scarring his iris, causing the brown pigment to darken into the colour of granite. Since then, the world had shown Chú Tùng's left eye its vulnerable side, one where all its edges were bubbling and fraying.

Dad was familiar with Chú Tùng from the time he also worked at Australia Post and it wasn't a good sign for Mum's fortune-teller pitch. 'Tùng?' Dad jeered, spraying bits of translucent melon, coriander and pork onto the sheet of plastic covering the table. 'The one with the stone eye and a head shaped like a taro? Real men don't visit fortune tellers.'

Chú Tùng also came along to a barbecue that my parents threw to celebrate my High Distinction in a creative writing competition run by the University of New South Wales. As he approached me by the smoky sticks of nem nướng, he winked and told me, 'You're a very smart girl but as a Buddhist, you should also know that impermanence permeates all aspects of life.' I'd thought about what he meant. The steel, rubber and plastic in the mail sorting facility were made to last for eternity – unlike its workers, Vietnamese refugees like him and my mother, who were made redundant when their bodies gave out. I held my golden certificate in both hands and closed my right eye. The certificate gleamed like a mirror and I saw my face reflected back to me, golden, my forehead tattooed with the words 'High Distinction'. Who cared what Chú Tùng, a sad man with a pathetic life, had to say?

Unlike Chú Tùng, Dad hadn't stayed at the Post long. 'Những ngày đen tối,' he labelled that period of his life. Day in, day out, sorting through mail, lugging sacks of parcels around, answering to some đầu gấu who growled bloody this, bloody that. Who didn't even graduate Year 12 and had a face pulled back like a snarling pit bull. After six months at Australia

Post, Dad had decided to go back to uni to study engineering. He wanted to be the guy he was back in Vietnam – working in a lab, running experiments and writing reports.

That wasn't an option for Mum, even though she had been a chemistry teacher at a girls' high school in Saigon. It was her duty to look after the baby. Me. Nicknamed Bé bí at the time because my skin was orange and my cheeks were sagging from being fed too much pumpkin. Apparently, I was always hungry. 'You would've drunk my blood if you could,' Mum told me. She'd stayed at Australia Post, becoming the temporary breadwinner in our family while Dad scaled back to part-time work to fit in his Masters degree.

Mum stood up to clear the dishes. Dad slurped the remains of his soup, his voice muffled by the rim of the bowl, 'Don't go paying some lunatic to tell you what your life will look like. That's what the hopeless and desperate do.' Turning to me, he put down the bowl and ruffled my hair, 'Con gái, get into a selective high school and your future will be secured.'

I felt all the bitter melon, pork and rice gurgle back up my throat. I'd failed the Department of Education's Opportunity Class test two years earlier and my parents thought that meant their daughter was doomed to be opportunity-less in the regular public education system. At the last parent–teacher night, however, Dad's hopes had been raised. Miss Carrington had informed him that I had the vocabulary of a seventeen-year-old and that my winning entry for the school's creative writing prize, a story about a clock that could talk, was 'suspiciously brilliant'. After reading it, she had contemplated calling my father to ask him not to help me with my homework but stopped short of doing so because she remembered that he 'probably wasn't capable' of helping his daughter with a creative writing assignment. Therefore, Miss Carrington believed that I was a 'truly gifted' child, and she would 'gladly consider' providing me with 'advanced homework'.

My father's reaction to Miss Carrington's back-handed compliment was worthy of a Logie. His tanned fingers loosened the tie around his neck. His eyeballs expanded and he leaned back in the plastic chair to stop Miss Carrington from seeing that he was actually rolling them. At the engineering consultancy where he worked as a hydrogeologist, Dad's manager, Bradley, banned him from presenting to clients because of his accent. After this incident, reading the *Macquarie Dictionary* on the weekend was a mandated activity in our house, along with watching *ABC News* every night to mimic the way the newsreaders pronounced things, and a weekly visit to Bankstown Library where I had to borrow five books (three non-fiction and two fiction). On the weekends, my parents also sent me to numerous tutoring centres where teachers like Miss Carrington made a side income. In my father's words, I'd have to have been as 'thick as a buffalo' not to have developed the vocabulary of a seventeen-year-old. Still, he leaned forward, both palms sliding onto the desk between him and Miss Carrington and declared, 'My daughter is not a gifted child. Miss, you are a gifted teacher.' Then he reached into his briefcase to pull out a box of Guylian chocolates (half-price sticker carefully peeled off on the car ride to the school) and a thank-you card.

Tears leaked from Miss Carrington's bottle-cap-blue eyes. She took off her glasses and wiped her face with the sleeve of her fuzzy cardigan. 'Mr Le, you are welcome. It is wonderful to finally be appreciated,' she said, blonde eyelashes wet.

The following week, Miss Carrington did give me advanced homework. She pulled me aside after class and thrust stapled pages in my face. They were a reading list called 'The Premier's Reading Challenge'. At the very top of the list was a book titled *Tomorrow When the War Began* by an author named John Marsden. I was interested in it because there was a Vietnamese–Thai character in the book named Lee, but I stopped reading after Lee made a joke about cooking 'sweet and sour possum' and 'feral cat dim sums'. That line reminded me of the time Clinton Ferrari lobbed one of my mum's spring rolls through a hole in the cricket nets on Harmony

Day. I abandoned the novel inside the concrete pipe in the playground and kept these thoughts to myself.

After Mum's failed pitch to raise funds and transportation services for a visit to the fortune teller, she stood at the sink and scrubbed the porcelain extra hard. Dad pushed open the flyscreen door to the backyard and poured a khaki mixture of leftover bitter melon soup and bits of dry dog food into Benny's bowl. Benny was our brown Lhasa Apso with floppy grey ears. Mum named him after Benny Stokes at work who called her Sweet Chilli – a smartass take on Chi Le, the name printed on her pass. She liked the idea of a Benny waiting on her for food and water, responding to her call immediately, running around in circles trying to gain her approval and affection. After all, that's what she had to spend eight hours a day doing for the Benny at work. Mum made sure that Benny the dog only answered to Vietnamese. She also made sure to pay her union fees on time.

The mystic lived in Fairfield, a fifteen-minute drive down the Hume Highway from our house in Yagoona. Mum and her work friend Bác Lan planned the visit for a Saturday evening when Bác Lan's husband and my father would be attending a drink-up at another Viet uncle's house. Neither Dad nor Bác

Lan's husband knew about this potentially life-altering visit. On Friday night, Bác Lan called our home phone. Dad picked up, turned to us and said, 'Chi, Lan wants to know if you two are still going over for a haircut tomorrow.' It was a good cover. Aside from being a mail officer, Bác Lan also ran a makeshift cash-only hair salon out of the old shed in her backyard: $12 for women; $10 for men.

The following evening, Mum and I sat on the steps of our front veranda waiting for Bác Lan. We'd finished an early dinner and Dad had already left the house. The sun was beginning to set. Blue, pink and yellow swirled together in the sky like a Paddle Pop. Above the pine tree in our front yard, the moon was clearly visible – a full bowl of congee floating past the spindly, deep-green branches that cockatoos perched on.

Bác Lan arrived in a faded gold Honda Civic outside the white fence with scalloped edges that surrounded our front yard. She honked the horn and watched us from behind oval glasses that made her look like a giant moth. We rattled down the highway until Bác Lan took a fast right turn into Horsley Drive. As the whole car leaned on its side, the scrunchie of synthetic brown hair came off her topknot. I dug my fingernails into the seat and felt my stomach lurching towards my ribcage. Mum screamed and gripped the armrest with her bony hands, her knuckles bulging like popcorn. The little jade

Buddha on her necklace slipped out of her shirt and swung in the air, smacking into a similar Buddha figurine hanging from the Honda's rear-view mirror. Thanks to the double Buddha blessing, the Honda thudded back into place.

The streets of Fairfield were so wide that you could fit our whole house in the middle of the road. A whole lot of Viets lived there. I could tell because banana trees were allowed to grow freely without the neighbours calling in Channel 9's *A Current Affair*. With leaves shaped like long feathers, the banana trees looked like giant pigeons thrusting their wings against a sky made of navy muslin. The mystic's house was less exciting – a beige fibro box that appeared too small for the square plot of land that it was on. The grass in the front yard came up to my waist and there were rusty car parts stacked against either side of the house. 'Housing commission,' my mum muttered under her breath. Her thin lips curled backwards and she sucked on her teeth. She was right. If the mystic was so successful, why did she live in such a dump?

I didn't know what housing commission meant but it was the same term Mum and Dad used to classify the house in Bevo that my great aunt Dì Tư lived in. My favourite thing in Dì Tư's house was the brown velvet couch in front of a cube-shaped TV that played images threaded with quivering fluoro-green lines. The last time we'd visited her for dinner, she'd made duck curry. In white ceramic bowls lined with navy, cubes of brown meat swam in a thick red broth dotted with translucent golden circles of fat. In the middle of our meal, Dì Tư took out a syringe with a bright orange tip from the pocket of her dressing gown and lifted her sweatshirt to reveal soft caramel skin folding in on itself. She plunged the needle into one of the folds on her stomach. Clear, viscous liquid chased by a black rubber stopper disappeared into Dì Tư's stomach. She burped loudly and put the needle back into her pocket. A piece of duck dived out of my mouth and plopped into the lake of red liquid in my bowl.

'Inh-su-linh cho đi-a-bê-ti-s,' Dì Tư explained, sliding a tissue in my direction.

On the way home, Dad wound down the front window of the car, letting fumes from the Hume Highway expunge any germs that may have clung onto us at Dì Tư's house. 'Another ugly mouth on welfare! She's been in the country longer than us, still can't speak any English and still relies on the government, on our taxes!' he bellowed, the syllables in each of his words diced by the gushes of air funnelling into the car. I felt my fringe split over my bare forehead and closed my eyes as the cool wind bathed my brain. I imagined that we were riding in one of the black choppers that often flew over our suburb, the ones my dad was personally offended by. 'Dô dụng,' my dad spat before winding up his window. I'd heard him say those words before, especially when I took too long learning how to calculate sums. Dô + Dụng = Useless.

On the front door of the mystic's house, a palm-sized mirror in a hexagonal red wooden frame hung from a rusty nail. Its shiny, warped surface reflected the moon. I tugged at the sleeve of Mum's denim jacket. 'Look, Mẹ, she's got the moon guarding her house. Why don't we ask Ba for one?'

'It's not a toy that you can play with and throw away when it breaks! It wards off evil spirits,' she snapped and pulled her jacket out of my clutches before knocking. The reverberation from each knock travelled to the red thread at the top of the mirror. The rusty nail wobbled and the mirror fell off, leaping towards me like a terrified animal. I caught it in my bare hands. Up close, I discovered that the hexagonal frame wasn't made of wood, but of the thick type of cardboard that I got from the Reject Shop for school projects.

I cradled the mirror in my palms and looked into it. I saw a face with two teeny eyes and a nose that bulged out like a pear. I was so shocked that I started touching my own face. The mirror showed my finger tracing along the blob-fish mouth that stretched out beneath the pear nose. How could this be my face? My dad had assured me that I had 'big eyes for a Viet' and a 'high nose bridge for a Viet'. He even told me that had I been born with monolid eyes and a flat nose, he would have saved up money to 'fix' both. He'd already put aside six grand for an orthodontist to straighten my teeth once I got a bit older. Both of my front teeth jutted in because I sucked on them whenever I was nervous. My canines popped out so much that when I closed my mouth too quickly, their pointy ends pressed on my lower lip. Looking into the little hexagonal mirror, I opened my lips slightly and saw my canines elongated like fangs. Just like a vampire. I wanted to alert Mum, but she'd already told me off for being annoying earlier.

The door was opened by a Vietnamese woman barely taller than my mother but wider than all three of her visitors put together. She stood there, hips almost touching each side of the doorway, glaring at us with black eyes and a flaky wart on her lip. Was she the Thầy bói or was she the receptionist of this fortune-telling business? I had imagined that she would at least be wearing circle sunglasses. In *Vân Sơn*, a direct-to-video Vietnamese–American comedy showcase that was passed around the Australia Post community via bootleg VHS, sketches depicted male fortune tellers as conniving swindlers who always had a pencil moustache, a pair of John Lennon–style sunglasses and a khăn đống – a black cloth turban. The closest things this woman had to any of that were some faint black hairs around the sides of her mouth.

We followed her down the hallway. Her bottom wobbled inside her grey sweatpants and there was a bald spot the size of a twenty-cent coin near the top of her scalp. Her feet were unexpected: small, round and white like the six-for-two-dollars dinner rolls at Coles, tiny toenails painted red and glossy like strawberry jam.

'How are you today, Thầy?' Bác Lan asked. I was surprised by the way Bác Lan addressed the tracksuit-wearing mystic. Thầy means teacher, but I'd only heard it used for men. My fingers curled around the demon-deterring door mirror, warping its cardboard edges. Không, this woman could not be a teacher. She looked like the witches in Vietnamese fairytales and her house stank of mothballs and cigarettes. She lived like my great aunt Dì Tư, who was a useless member of society.

We ended up in a room where the walls were each adorned with a giant version of the mirror I held in my hand: four metre-wide red hexagons, each with a perfectly circular mirror in the middle. Sets of gold lines had been painted onto the walls surrounding each hexagon, giving the impression of a ripple effect spreading out through the room. In the middle of the floor was a wooden, glass-topped table, also hexagonal and surrounded by hexagonal cushions. The mystic sank into one of the cushions and lit up a cigarette. Mum and Bác Lan sat opposite her, each taking up a side of the table. I stood there, bare toes tickled by the fuzzy orange carpet, not wanting to sit next to the mystic. I stared into the hexagon mirror to my left. The same teeny-tiny eyes, flat nose and fangs. I wanted to kick, cry and scream, but I also just wanted to see what would happen next. If I could win another creative writing trophy at school for writing about this, it would be worth the fangs and the flat nose.

'Bé!' the mystic rasped, clapping her hands in my direction and pointing to a cushion beside her. It was disgusting being addressed as *baby* by this cane toad. Mum fumbled through her Benny-sized handbag and pulled out a parcel wrapped in a page from last week's *Việt Luận*. Inside, she counted four twenty-dollar bills. She rubbed them between her thumb and index finger, making sure she had the right number of notes.

Bác Lan dropped her pudgy hand on my mum's shoulder, 'Chi, let's see what she says first.' Mum stuffed the package back into her navy canvas bag and pushed it in my direction. I pulled the sack onto my lap and rummaged through it looking for bubblegum. In there was the rest of last week's *Việt Luận* (the front-page story was about a Viet kid who achieved a 100 UAI and was accepted into Medicine at USYD), a fluoro-green plastic comb that Mum liked to rake through her puffy mushroom bob cut and a half-used Revlon lipstick the rusty old-blood colour of sarsaparilla.

Thầy bói shuffled her pack of cards with a Criss Angel level of agility. Black clubs and red diamonds flashed in a blur of laminated cardboard. I was disappointed – this lady had giant hexagons installed on the walls, but the actual work came down to flipping playing cards from the Reject Shop? I was certain these cards were just the regular ones, the type I saw at my cousin's house during Tết. My father didn't let me participate in their games. He told me it was *đánh bài* and that Viets like Dì Tư already had enough problems from being addicted to it.

'Remember,' Dad said. '*Đánh bài* means *gambling* and it's one tiny mark away from *đánh bại* – *defeat*.' It was rich coming from a man who entered the Powerball every week but I appreciated learning about these little games in the Vietnamese language.

Too bad I could not use these lessons to win more creative writing awards. Nobody who judged the awards at school could understand Vietnamese. Once, when the recess bell rang, I'd hung back in the demountable classroom and approached Miss Carrington at her desk, 'Miss, did you know that in Vietnamese, *sáng ăn khoai* means you have to eat taro for breakfast but if you switch it around to *khoái ăn sáng*, it means you love to eat breakfast?'

Miss Carrington's blue eyes darted to her watch. 'Oh sweetie, when the first syllables or letters of words are swapped, that's called a spoonerism. A spoonerism is also a mistake.'

I clamped my canines down on my bottom lip and nodded. Then I pulled my school hat onto my head to cover my red ears and left Miss Carrington to eat the soggy and sulphurous egg salad sandwich on her desk in peace. How could it be a mistake? Having taro for breakfast meant that you were too poor to afford rice or noodles, but a simple switch of two syllables reminded you to be grateful for even having a breakfast to eat. There were plenty of things in English that didn't make sense to me and my family, like why the *h* in *honest* is silent or how *buckle* could have contradictory meanings like 'to break down' or 'to secure'. We accepted these aberrations as rules. Each time we came across a new rule, we twisted our tongues, moulded our minds and broke our backs to meet the standard.

Bác Lan's future was being told first. *Phluck*. With a sweep of her salon-standard strawberry nails, Thầy bói laid out a pile of cards on the glass table. *Phluck. Phluck. Phluck*. And then there were three more piles. Her upper lip, goanna thin, twitched like it was trying to dislodge the wart resting on it. Why couldn't Thầy bói just forgo some manicure sessions and put the money towards freezing off that wart? She coughed like TV static before reading out the cards on top of each pile, 'Ace of Spades, Queen of Khhhhhearts, Jokhhhhher and five of Khhhhhhclubs.' Mum's left hand fluttered towards her jade Buddha. Bác Lan rested her big head on her right hand, which she cupped under her chin as if already resigned to the fate laid out in the cards before her. Thầy bói leaned forward, fingers steepled like Mr Burns'. 'The next generations are a gift, not a burden.'

A single tear trickled from Bác Lan's right eye. It slid down her cheek, taking with it some white pigment from the layer of powder on her skin. Mum reached over and took one of Bác Lan's hands into her own. Two months ago, our family had attended a party at Bác Lan's house that was really a wedding between Xuân, Bác Lan's pregnant sixteen-year-old daughter, and Long, the seventeen-year-old Viet boy who had knocked her up. The occasion was so controversial that my parents fought about whether or not to go up until the last minute.

'If we go, that means we're celebrating something wrong and disgusting,' Mum muttered from the back seat of the Holden.

Dad twisted his body away from the steering wheel and turned to face Mum. 'Xuân stabbed her parents in the heart with her whoring ways and now you want to shoot them in the face with your disloyalty?' He glared at her like a stone dragon at the temple.

At the teen wedding, there was a suckling pig slowly rotating on a spit roast placed near the swimming pool in Bác

Lan's backyard. Rivers of translucent fat trickled from the cracks in its red lacquered skin. On the wooden kitchen table inside the house was a giant durian sponge cake covered in whipped cream bearing the words 'Congratulations Xuân and Long' in red cursive. Xuân waddled around the house in a sparkling white muumuu that draped over her bulging stomach. She still had her signature look: waist-length hair dyed a deep cherry red and a tiny blue crystal impaled through her left nostril. Her face, once oval, was so bloated that the tops of her cheeks squished the bags under her eyes. Her baby daddy, Long, was shaped like a snake bean, jeans past his pikelet arse and an oversized hoodie, hood pulled up and tucked behind a spiky gate of gelled hair.

In the mystic's cramped living room, Bác Lan tried to pull herself together. She took a deep breath in, pulled back her shoulders and tightened the fake hair scrunchie on her bun. 'What else do you see?' she asked.

'Dragons are slippery creatures, don't try to hold onto them,' Thầy bói replied.

Dragons in Vietnamese culture were not the same as the fire breathing Norbert in *Harry Potter* or the greedy Smaug in *The Lord of the Rings*. Lạc Long Quân was a dragon king who rose from the depths of the ocean and fell in love with Âu Cơ, a fairy goddess who lived in the mountains.

They married, laid one hundred eggs and out of those eggs hatched the first Vietnamese people. Little did they know that thousands of years later, new dynasties of Vietnamese people would be born all over the world. Long, a second-generation Vietnamese–Australian boy raised on Tupac, T5 and tabouli had impregnated Xuân, a second-generation Vietnamese–Australian girl who knew the words to every Spice Girls song and who taught me how to fold stars out of pastel strips of paper. The next generation of mixed-up Viets from mixed-up places who spoke mixed-up languages was already here. Like, way too soon. Bác Lan had wanted Xuân to finish university and then get married and have kids. A sixteen-year-old pregnant Vietnamese girl was not *progress*.

At the wedding, when everyone had gathered around the table for speeches, Long's mates from Birrong Boys had shoved his face into the cake. 'Ahhh fucckkkinell boyz!' Long's grinning head emerged from the mushy mess. Sunny morsels of durian were impaled on his hair spikes and foamy globs of whipped cream dripped from his chin to form a beard. Any parent who'd named their child Long had higher hopes for him. On the drive back to our house, Dad had taken the opportunity to give me a lecture: 'Xuân's destroyed her future. Having a great career *and* a baby is what you need to aim for.' Mum sat so still that it was like she'd dissolved into the night.

Sitting on Thầy bói's hexagonal cushion was giving my legs pins and needles. As I massaged my shins, I wondered if her predictions meant that Xuân and Long would end up like our ancestors. According to a book on Vietnamese fairy tales that I'd borrowed from Bankstown Library, Long and Âu Cơ did not have a traditional happily ever after. Long took fifty children back to the sea and Âu Cơ took fifty children into the mountains. That's basically divorce and shared custody – suddenly a no-no thousands of years later. I didn't want to embarrass Bác Lan by looking at her directly, so I turned my head and looked at her reflection in one of the mirrors. I saw ashy shadows flickering under Bác Lan's eyes and noticed that her reflection did not show the synthetic hair scrunchie or sequin-embroidered cardigan she was wearing. Instead, Bác Lan appeared tired and plain with grey hairs showing in her topknot and soft arms peeking from a white singlet. None of her facial features were distorted. Why was I the only one with pea-sized eyes and fangs? Bác Lan's single tear had escalated into sobbing.

'Con gái, tissue.' Mum pointed at me and then at her purse, which lay near the small hexagonal mirror I'd brought into the house.

I fished out a squashed packet of tissues in the inner pocket of the purse and yanked a thick wad out of the plastic cover.

I passed it to Mum. Bác Lan blew her nose into the tissue so hard that when she removed her hand, her nose was bright red. Thầy bói had not moved out of her steepled-fingers pose. Her mouth was a line carved in concrete and her eyes were made of asphalt. How could she sit there and watch poor Bác Lan having a meltdown? She was either a witch or a man. Thầy bói croaked and flicked her head towards her next victim. I didn't know why Mum was bothering to have her fortune read. I didn't get into an Opportunity Class but I made up for it by being top of my class at school. Or was she worried that I would end up like Xuân?

Mum rubbed Bác Lan's back before returning her attention to the hexagonal table.

Phluck. Thầy bói worked faster this time, fingers blurring like a human pokie machine. *Phluck. Phluck. Phluck.* Her upper lip twitched again and the wart attached to it wobbled. 'King of Clubs, Joker, Two of Diamonds and Ace of Spades.'

Mum wrapped a fist around her jade Buddha pendant. Bác Lan peered over a wad of tissues, her eyeballs rimmed red. Was she going to report the findings to every Viet at Australia Post tomorrow morning?

'You're going to regret living with vampires.' Thầy bói leaned back and fished a cigarette out of one back pocket of her tracksuit pant and a lighter out of the other. Vampire? Was she referring to me? This welfare-guzzling gargoyle had gone too far. I turned to my mother, expecting her to be enraged on my behalf. Instead, her shoulders were slumped. She looked down at the callouses on her fingers and let out a sigh. Bác Lan's eyebrows were knitted together in confusion but she comforted Mum by patting her on the back anyway.

Thầy bói turned to me, eyes softened, looking more human than she'd looked all night. 'Smart little girl, why don't you look at your mother's reflection?' I turned to the mirror opposite Mum. A young woman with large wire spectacles and long straight hair flowing past the mandarin collar of a white áo dài smiled back at me. I'd seen this woman before. A photo of her was perched on the bedside drawer that contained my mother's black-velvet jewellery box. It was Mum when she graduated with her chemistry degree from the University of Saigon, ready to be a teacher. I imagined that she loved doing experiments with chemicals and elements that fizzed and bubbled. She met Dad on the way to work after he'd rammed into her bicycle with a moped. I looked at Mum now, all the vitality and ambition sucked out of her.

'I already do,' Mum replied to the mystic, her voice so low that it seemed to reverberate around the room. I tugged my mother's jacket but she remained still and calm like Buddha. I wanted to go home because if we went home, Mum would forget about the reflection in that mirror and she could go back to being my mother, scolding me for breaking things and telling me interesting stories about faraway places and faraway people.

Bác Lan reached under the table, pulled out the wrapped-up cash and pushed it across the table in a movement like ripping a bandaid off a wound. Bác Lan and Mum held onto each other as they stood up from the cushions.

On the way out of the mystic's house, I handed back the little hexagonal mirror that had fallen off her front door. I had considered keeping it as a souvenir of this adventure but didn't see the value in having something that made me feel so ugly. Thầy bói took the mirror with both hands and grinned at me so widely that the wart on her upper lip touched the bottom of her nostril. 'You'll figure it out, little girl. Good stories always have great riddles.' I rolled my eyes at her, the rudest thing I could do as a child to an adult. She, a houso and a swindler, was no teacher of mine.

COMMUNITIES OF CONCERN

Sara M Saleh

'How much longer must we wait, ya3ni?' Aunty Mahasen scowled. 'Till our funerals?' Her white square handkerchief bounced around in her hand, reminiscent of an Umm Kulthum performance. Although her glossy lips were pursed in an attempted whisper, her voice boomed like a Friday-night football broadcaster's. Thankfully, we were the only ones seated at Table 36.

'It's Sahar's fault for bringing us here so early like we have nothing better to do,' Aunty Nabila chimed in snidely. Her long, thin tattooed eyebrows arched across her forehead in what looked like an infinite line. She glared at me but I shifted in my cushioned chair so the giant centrepiece of fake blush roses and leafy greens blocked her view.

I hated how OTT our Leb weddings were. How the whole village showed up like Australia's own Lebanon, ready to celebrate everyone and complain about everything. Deep down though, I did love the nauseating stockpile of tulle and diamantes and Arab aunties and fireworks and chicken mushroom and tablehs.

'And what about these seats, are we the help?' Aunty

Mahasen added, her voice jumping a decibel with each word, the handkerchief helplessly flailing about again. 'This is worse than that table we bought for Nancy's concert. Took out a mortgage to sit in the car park.'

'I am sorry, I didn't mean for us to arrive so early.' My attempts to temper the conversation felt like trying to shove an oversized knit sweater into an overflowing drawer. I quickly skimmed the surroundings to check if anyone had overheard us, but we were safe, other guests absorbed in their own chatter. 'Murphy's Law, huh?' The pair glanced at me puzzled, with Aunty Nabila's meter-long line of a brow forming a zigzag.

The month before, we had been horrifyingly late to Rawan's wedding – a combination of weekend M5 congestion and my aunts' diligent observance of EST (Ethnic Standard Time). But on our drive to the Bellevue that Sunday afternoon, the motorway had been deserted.

'Bala curfew, bala curfew! To hell with this curfew!' Aunty Mahasen had said exasperatedly, reading my mind. 'As if that's going to solve anything.' With the number of cases in our areas rapidly rising, the government had announced a curfew, which was to start the next day. But this wedding had been on our social calendar for months, and to my aunties, missing a Leb wedding meant excommunication.

Where is she? I checked my phone for messages. My

stepsister Zeynab had no doubt anticipated what the illuminated digits on the screen confirmed: we were definitely not going to be starting on time.

'You know, they have so many relatives,' Aunty Nabila restarted the commentary with the serious and self-important expression of a *Today Tonight* presenter. 'But I heard the family overseas couldn't make it. All their visas got rejected.'

'Yiii, haram. El farha na'asa. How sad for them,' Aunty Mahasen replied as she took a swig of fizzy cola. I eyed the way she had tied her navy scarf around her oval face, like she was about to farewell sailors at the harbour. 'Anyway,' she went on. 'Since we're not *close* close, I'd say this table is decent, ma heik? We have a screen right behind us and we're next to the kitchen, so we'll get fed first.' I smiled, appreciating her order of priorities and the fact that she had reached that conclusion all on her own.

A splash of colour caught my attention, the scarlet hue demanding to be seen before I realised the gown belonged to Zeynab. She was still a few metres away but I stood to greet her, careful not to make any sudden movements. My own dress had me feeling like a stuffed shrimp taco. I adjusted the satin, smoothing it out over my belly and hips. 'Sahar!' Zeynab grabbed my hand and air kissed me to avoid smudging the layers of coppers and caramels on her face, her cinnamon-bark skin iridescent under the harsh hall light. She inspected me closely and wiggled her bushy brows. 'Auuuunties!' she bleated, turning to face them. 'Wow! Kardashian who? You are both dazzling mashaAllah!' She ignored my eye rolls and continued, slowly enunciating each word. 'Don't go breaking any hearts tonight!' Zeynab might have been an Australian-born South African, but she was fluent in Ethnic Migrant Aunty. They both tipped their heads back in rehearsed humility and high-pitched giggles. Zeynab grinned, pleased with herself.

'Lips emoji, peach emoji,' I said, shaking my head.

'Did this venue shrink since our last time here?' Aunty Mahasen's white handkerchief was back up again as she reached for a handful of roasted nuts from the glass bowl in front of her. Her face shrivelled in disgust. 'Stale.'

'Zeynab!' I beckoned her over to my side of the table before Aunty Mahasen, emboldened by her new audience member, could launch into another rant. Zeynab plopped herself on the chair next to me.

'Sooo … have you seen him yet?'

'Whooo?' *So much for blasé, more like highly strung owl.* I smacked my lips together as if reapplying lipstick and craned my neck, casually taking in the hall. It had filled up with tantes in towering turbans and 3ammos in ill-fitting suits, young women in block-coloured bandage bodycons and young men sporting Tarocash bowties in varying polka-dot patterns. The dance floor divided the room, which had been set up to accommodate 500 guests – 480 of them probably from the Leb side. Each table was topped with the same fake-rose centrepiece and lined with an assortment of favours: *Steve & Dalia* embossed fondant biscuits, pink almond sugars and chocolates in metallic foil, all bundled in netting and tied with cream ribbons. The dance floor had strings and strings of green vines and fairy lights dangling low from the canopy overhead. On the stage was the kosha, the extravagant gilded throne where the bride and groom would sit, before a backdrop of plush maroon velvet curtains. Ivory cloths were draped over the table in front, and empty sparkling flutes stood waiting to be filled with what I assumed would be fake but extra bubbly champagne. It resembled every other wedding we had been to recently. Clearly the bride's Leb side had won out over the groom's White side.

'Sahar? Is that how you're playing this? Ignoring my question?' Zeynab's voice brought me back to Table 36. 'Well, you know what can't be ignored? You. In that dress. The way it fits after all these years!' She outlined a bottle with her palms, her Riri-inspired orange stiletto acrylics flickering like neon lights.

'Shhhhh!' My eyes signalled towards my aunties. 'It doesn't

get more halal than this,' I appealed to her, motioning to my long, loose emerald satin sleeves.

'Yea. You're all about that halal life tonight.'

I stifled a laugh. Until that moment, my head had been a whirlpool of anxieties: the job interview that Monday (which was at the community legal centre where Zeynab temped, and which I desperately needed to ace) and making rent, the impending curfew and what that could lead to (Muslim bans, checkpoints, camps all seemed like a real-world possibility) and … seeing *him* for the first time since our breakup.

'Speaking of,' Zeynab said. 'I need to tell you something more on the haram side later tonight. Nothing serious.' Her sobered-up expression suggested otherwise, and I wondered whether all her energy that evening was because she was bursting to share some big news. I was intrigued.

'Zeynab, I —'

DUM-DA-DUM! DUM-DA-DUM. A drumbeat thudded and reverberated across the dimmed hall. My ears pulsed as a zumeyra streaked its way through the air. The bridal party had arrived. Zeynab and I jumped up, arching our necks towards the source of the commotion. At the entrance, a small troupe of men in white blouses and loose black pants, their long, dark hair tied back, began the zaffe: the music procession. My aunties, still seated, rotated their chairs to watch the zaffe on a little screen perched on the wall behind us. 'The screen is so small,' Aunty Nabila grumbled.

Steve and Dalia, along with their four bridesmaids dressed in shimmering shades of rose gold and four groomsmen with shiny rose-gold ties, made their way to the dance floor. A large crowd surrounded them, clapping and cheering, mobile phone torches and camera flashes punctuating the air. One of the drummers galloped enthusiastically into the centre of the circle – banging and galloping, galloping and banging. Fireworks started to spray out like confetti at the back of the floor just in front of the kosha. It was all so tacky. My eyes followed Dalia and Steve, who had clasped their hands in the air, shaking and shimmying back and forth, their shoulders in sync.

'Not bad for a White dude, huh!' Zeynab said.

I was too distracted by Dalia's coats of fake tan, the glowing stains visible across her upper body. My own inner judgy aunty was clawing her way out to liberation. The music volume lowered and a petite woman in a sparkling silver turban and wiry spectacles began to yell praises at the bride, complimenting her unparalleled beauty and wishing the couple a prosperous marriage. Each sentence by the screeching lady, who I assumed was Dalia's teta, was followed by a chorus of *aweeeeeehas* from the crowd. It reminded me of a slam poetry performance I'd seen at an open mic night in Granville, where most of the performers had shared pieces about racism and queerness and colonialism and climate change as audiences of all colours clicked and stomped and *mmm'd* enthusiastically. Zeynab had taken me; she was always looking for underground pockets like that, to meet more people like her. Even then, when Zeynab was young enough to be optimistic about things, she was mature enough, South African enough, to know that living on land that wasn't ours came with consequences. And though younger than me, she taught me to pay more attention to the world outside ourselves.

That was also the night I'd met Ali. Not at the slam – that was not his scene – but in line at EJs when we went to get chicken rolls after. Nothing says 'meant to be' like bonding over toum and pickles.

'Li-li-li-li-li!' a bunch of women ululated, summoning me back to the wedding. A slow instrumental piece floated out of the speakers. The circle of merry guests dissipated, and the bride and groom had their first slow dance to a generic Ed Sheeran song, the name of which I couldn't recall.

'Bet you Steve picked this,' Zeynab said.

'Bet you it's the only thing he got to pick in this entire wedding.'

The crowd hushed as a sweaty Steve twisted and spun

Dalia, her A-line floor-length dress half-heartedly twirling at the bottom. 'You call that a wedding dress?' Aunty Nabila sneered. 'It's a nightgown.' As she pointed fervently to Dalia, her bejewelled headband slipped back to reveal badly dyed roots.

'A curtain! Where are the beads? The sequins? Not even a single pearl!' Aunty Mahasen added, pursing her lips, her face inflating like a blowfish. 'Why is she dressing like the ajaneb now?'

Zeynab and I side-eyed each other smirking. I was surprised neither aunty had commented yet on Steve's outfit. He was not in the mandatory full suit, and his shirt was checked. To Arabs, this was blasphemy of the highest order.

'Time to get everyone on the dance floor!' The DJ interrupted, feigning enthusiasm in between vapes. Like all other attendees under forty, and a few overly enthusiastic elders, Zeynab was soon up on her feet, palms waving, upper body popping as she mouthed lyrics to 'I Follow Rivers' – a classic we both loved. I hesitated, not sure I was ready for the sticky, pushy mob, with each Hot Young Thing trying to outdo the next.

Zeynab shook her head. 'I am not having it. Tonight, we are dancing! I need to dance!' She was swaying in a way that made it impossible to reject her request.

I gingerly got up again, silently praying I had stretched

my dress out enough for some regular breathing. I still felt my diaphragm struggling for room as I followed Zeynab's lead through the tables towards the dance floor. While she glided through, I wiggled and writhed between chairs. *Why are they arranged so close together?*

'Hello, hello. Salam! Oh hi, hello! Salam!' I said, hoping to distract people as I struggled to squeeze myself through chairs. I chucked in a few polite nods to tantes and 3ammos who I didn't know enough to stop and engage in small talk. We were almost at the dance floor, where the crowd had split into groups: hips-don't-lie Lebs on one side; awkward White people on another; and try-hard Lebs and brave Whites in the middle. The music transitioned to the iconic opening of Nancy Ajram's 'Akhasmak ah'. Zeynab let out a squeal – she loved this Nancy song more than I did. As I shimmied and swung my arms, trying to match Zeynab's energy levels, I smacked something hard with the back of my hand. I turned around and a little girl in pigtails with yellow star stickers on her cheeks was holding her nose and squinting in pain.

Oh shit. 'I'm so sorry! Are you okay? I am so sorry.' I nervously grabbed her shoulder, petting the frills of her lilac taffeta dress. I needed to soothe her before any tears were shed and before any guests looked our way. Zeynab paused midway through her elaborate dance routine, her jaw hanging wide.

She sprang to my rescue and bent down so she was almost face-to-face with the girl.

'What's your name, sweetie? And what did this mean lady do to you?' she was half-yelling, in competition with Nancy's trills. The girl's face was crinkled, her small hand covering her nose. She sniffled, like she was still deciding whether to cry or not.

I looked around. *Thank God everyone is too busy dancing.* Suddenly, my entire body stiffened. A familiar cleft chin stood out from the sea of faces. It all came rushing back like shards of glass breaking in an emergency. Tablehs, venue disagreements, endless guest lists, menu choices and cake tasting, a half-assed apology, cancelled invitations, the prying phone calls and texts, the humiliation and the can't-get-out-of-bed sadness and bottomless tubs of cookie-dough ice cream.

Ali smiled, a smile that was half solidarity, half sympathy. It reminded me of how I sometimes smiled at Muslims and people of colour in the street. I sensed Ali had a front-row seat to my assault on the kid, who had finally decided to bawl her eyes out. I tore myself away from him and turned to Zeynab. 'I am so, so sorry.' My words stumbled out: 'I gotta go!' She didn't hear me as she asked the girl where her parents were. I left the dance floor and hurried to the entrance.

In the hallway, I was greeted by an easel with a huge portrait of Dalia smiling, her teeth outrageously white and luminescent, with Steve behind her, his arms wrapped around her waist. They were in matching baby-blue shirts with their names and the date superimposed across the canvas in sprawling gold-leaf cursive. It looked like one of those insipid real-estate ads with a Barbie-and-Ken-like couple posing in front of the suburban dream home they'd just purchased. How absurd. But, of course, Ali and I had planned to do the same thing. I marched, panting, down the familiar hallway to the bathrooms, my toes slipping as they adjusted to my rapid pace.

Ali and I didn't have any big dramatic fight. It wasn't an Egyptian soap opera. No *Majnun wa Layla* 2.0. The truth was more insidious. Australia ended us before we'd even got together. Australia, a sculptor with its chisel, chipped and chipped at us until we were no longer recognisable to each other. The more agitated I became about the events happening around us and to us, the more I wanted to do something about it. My change in career path meant long hours and late nights and time away from Ali, and this was too much change, a sacrifice he was unwilling to make.

'He thinks if we stayed quiet and stuck to our lanes, we would stay safe and maybe even live out "The Australian

Dream"', Zeynab had said at the time, as I let out sporadic sobs like a scratchy record. 'Doesn't he know, there is no dream? Not for our parents, not for us. But there can be for our children if we change things.'

As I pulled open the bathroom door, the thumping music faded and one hundred different perfumes assaulted my nose. A group of women in an array of animal prints – snake, zebra, tiger – paired with chunky bracelets, gaudy gem necklaces and statement earrings were absorbed in conversation.

'Is she half Leb or Leb Leb? I heard her mother is Palo?'

'She's got such fair skin, it's so beautiful. Like a polished pebble. No wonder she's managed to snag an ajnabi.'

'Apparently she spends a fortune on skin care.'

'I hear half of her is fake, Sis.'

It was like listening to Western Sydney's version of Cinderella's evil stepsisters. At that instant, a tall woman in an '80s-style velvet dress emerged from the cubicle with the resolve of a superhero appearing from a phonebooth after their costume change. *Velvet does nothing for our Arab bums*, I heard Aunt Mahasen saying in my head.

I was immediately struck by the woman's foam-green eyes in contrast with the auburn bob bordering her cheeks. Her small head floated between the puffy shoulder pads. Catching my disbelief, her eyes widened in an expression of camaraderie. Clearly, she too had been following the gossip sesh. After washing her slender hands at the sink, the tall woman shook them hard, a dog shaking the ocean off its coat. Droplets pelted the group of gossipers and they flocked out fuming, fumbling over each other like bowling pins.

Impressed, I bowed down to the woman in velvet, my superhero.

She laughed. 'I concede, that may have been a gross overreaction. But they deserved it.'

'At least wait until after the wedding to provide your detailed analysis that nobody asked for!' As I said this, my mind wandered to Table 36, where my aunties were likely complaining about something or the other.

'Exactly … not to mention that "Fair and Lovely" crock of shit. You'd think we'd be over that by now,' she exclaimed with a long sigh. 'Alright, comrade, time to go back out there and brave the jungle.'

'This food tastes like cardboard.' Aunty Mahasen's face crumpled as she chewed.

'More like rubber,' Aunty Nabila announced, a fork and knife in each hand as she scraped a piece of pale creamy chicken breast off her plate.

I exhaled loudly. Zeynab popped up, somehow still immaculate despite her earlier dance-floor shenanigans. I beckoned for her to eat, pointing to the extra plates of food. Presumably the other guests assigned to Table 36 were a no-show, or didn't want to sit next to my aunties.

'The carrots! The carrots taste like plastic,' Aunty Mahasen muttered to herself, clearing her throat before shovelling another baby carrot into her mouth.

'I need to go, uh, powder my cheeks,' Zeynab said. 'Join me?'

'Is this about that thing you wanted to tell me? Listen, if it's Ali, I already spotted him and I really don't care. I'm fine, I'm fiiine.' I shrugged. *There, nailed the casual nonchalant tone this time.*

'No, no.' She looked me in the eye, her neon-lit hands pleading with me to stop.

We were the only ones in the hallway as we walked past the real-estate ad/wedding photoshoot and back towards the bathroom. Zeynab swung open the doors and checked the empty insides.

'Okay. What's going on?' My heart raced. If it wasn't Ali, was it work? Did she know something? That interview had been a Hail Mary. Zeynab, like a magician with a bottomless black top hat, unzipped her purse and pulled out a grey and pink thermometer. She handed it to me and quietly stared into the mirror, avoiding eye contact. I squinted at the plus sign in the little window of what I was realising was not a thermometer. 'Is that what I think it is?' I asked, my confusion cutting across the quiet. It was the first time I'd seen a pregnancy test, let alone registered that its owner was my stepsister and best friend.

'Speaking of haram. Ha. Ha,' Zeynab said meekly, biting her bronzed bottom lip. 'I was sick this morning and it didn't occur to me until I was on my way here that I'm ten days late. I stopped and bought the test. I couldn't wait.'

'Oh my God … are you … are you okay? And … how did … I mean I know how … but … how? What?' My mind swarmed as I struggled to think of what to say. I wanted to ask about the father, but my mouth was suddenly dry – a mixture of pleasant shock, cautious happiness, searing curiosity and over-protective panic.

'The father is not important.' There was Zeynab with her Jedi mind tricks. 'I guess … there's a lot to think about. I'm doing this solo, as an Unmarried Muslim Woman. And I know with everything going on, the curfew, your interview, Ali, it's just really bad timing …' Her voice trailed off, her gaze lowering to the floor.

'No, stop, don't say that.' I felt like I was seeing her for the first time all night, and yet, inexplicably, it was like I'd already known all along. Our weddings had a way of inciting realisations before we could even name them. 'Okay. Okay. We can do this together.' I caressed her arm with one hand, the other clutching the test. 'Oh. I just realised I am still holding your pee.'

She snorted softly. 'I'm scared, Sahar. Absolutely no one can find out. I don't want to be the hot goss for the next five years!'

'Well, we better get out of here then, avoid this hotbed of aunty activity at all costs.'

Almost prophetically, the bathroom door swung open, banging the wall behind it. An older lady with a pearl-studded black hijab whom I recognised as Tante Fathiya, one of my aunties' closest friends, sauntered into the bathroom. Noticing me, Tante Fathiya approached, as though she was about to say her salams. She then took one glance at the pregnancy test in my hand and jolted backwards, gasping loudly to the Almighty and pirouetting on her heels towards the exit. Zeynab and I stared at each other, limp in place, two lambs on Eid morning.

'Eemmm … I guess you won't have to worry about that anymore, Z!' Stunned, I walked out of the bathroom and left Zeynab behind. I dashed back to the table before the headline could make its way down the Aunty Newswire. As soon as I stepped into the hall, Aunty Nabila grabbed me by the torso with the grip of a wrestler. Damn. The Newswire was more efficient than ever. 'You're late!' she scolded, thrusting me into the centre of the dance floor where all the young women at the wedding congregated. 'Don't want to miss the bouquet toss!' Aunty yelled after me, her badly dyed roots stark under the dance floor lights. I smiled helplessly, feeling trapped in a bowl but thankful I was temporarily alive and well.

Dalia, with her tan stains and nightgown dress, stood like a teacher at the front of her classroom. 'Are you readyyyy?' she screamed, swirling her thick blush-and-green bouquet over her tight chignon, still intact hours later thanks to an entire bottle of extra-strong-hold hairspray. I looked towards the bathroom door – no sign of Zeynab – then searched the crowd for a way out, a way to prevent Aunty Fathiya from airing the news. Then my gaze landed on a face: my bathroom superhero in the '80s velvet dress. She was standing next to a man with a familiar cleft chin. She squeezed Ali's hand, as if there was an inside joke between them, before joining the dance floor. She spotted me and winked. My mouth reflexively stretched out so wide I felt my lips crack like plaster. The image of Tante Fathiya walking in on us like a gust of wind, of Zeynab's look of dread, dissolved from my mind. *I am going to get the bouquet and a shrapnel of dignity along with it.*

As I swivelled, Dalia yelled something in the background

and a bunch of girls screamed, diving towards me. Whack! The bouquet hit me in the face like a rogue coconut then landed at my feet. Fluttering my lids through the sharp discomfort, I finally located Tante Fathiya, who was standing like a preacher amongst a throng of tantes gasping and shaking their heads. I could almost see the ripple of scandal spreading through the wedding like a wildfire.

This news is bigger than the Western Sydney curfew … It then dawned on me that this last celebration together for who knew how long was going to be the talk of town for months, but for all the wrong reasons. I raised a hand to my face, which was still stinging, and thought of the little crying girl I'd abandoned on the floor earlier. My pregnant stepsister who I'd left wallowing in the bathroom. I definitely deserved that hit to the head.

SONG OF THE FROG

Omar Musa

ha ha – you could say i earned these stripes – black on
yellow,
each one unique as the fingerprints of the men whose
hands gripped
musket and spade, each stripe unique as the snowflakes
that fall soft
around us final few – ha haaaa – i creak my gallows
laughter out into
the long, snowy dark, out, over the creeks and granite
tors, the florets of
moss like slow stellar explosions, my song scrapes along
the valleys and
rock floors searching for purchase, nocturne for my
ravaged clutch and
rangy beloved – the stripes on his belly were cornflower
blue, we fed
each other upland psalms and buried our eyes in the stars
above the land.

first it was brumbies, then it was the pigs.

even before the men, into our world rampaged those
bundles of muscle and tusk,
hoof, hot breath and nostril, slicing up turf and tussock,
shitting on our heads,
chewing up our sphagnum to shit on us again,
forewarning of the pale men whose
frostbitten words slalom down the icy crevasses and
fallen snow gums – they
redirect history and dam a world, the turbines turn and
warm their homes, our homes
interned, warmed, in turn, like turning globe, burning,
heating up like fresh powder on
dinnerplate in a microwave, crushed up by credit card in
alpine lodge, it is snow season
in more ways than one – haa haaaa, i'm the funny one
again – if you can't laugh, you die.

before they had their pandemic, we had ours – were are
losing our minds – our skin crawls with devils – no
one can say from whence it came, we spread madness
to each other – there is another world where this
never occurred – but in this world, we are held in

shipping containers – all straight lines – our only
hope – by creatures with test tubes, microscopes and
underfunded visions – we have more in common with
them than might first appear – they, like us, are not
believed – like us, a dying breed.

you can hold me in your palm – *dazed* – i can hold
you in my eye – blink once if you're being held
against your will, you say – in one blink – *blink* – a
millennium becomes a matter of days —

HA HAAA
WE FED
EACH OTHER
UPLAND
PSALMS

A A A
A
A
A!
AND BURIED
OUR EYES IN THE
STARS ABOVE
THE
LAND

PAPER THIN

Anne-Marie Te Whiu

Beside Mum's bed was a little table with a drawer that had things like tissues and puffers, a jar of Vicks and a tube of Amolin, which she'd squeeze and rub over her lips and under her nose until they shone. These were the smells of my childhood. Nights were often hard for Mum. Her body lay on the bed but her lungs wanted to leave her chest. Asthma attacks were frequent visitors. A small white plate also sat on the table and it held a special ring as well as a fine gold necklace. Mum would pick up the necklace to wear and usually it would be knotted tight in several places. I used to love undoing those knots. I'd hold the chain up close, inspecting each bind. It was beautiful and frustrating to see the way the loops turned back on each other. A talent I had as a kid was undoing these knots. My tiny hands could do the work. It felt so good undoing it, passing it to Mum, her necklace all evened out – it was a little way of telling Mum that I loved her. I made her chain knotless.

For most of my adult life there has been a rope of knots that I have not been able to undo. This particular rope has been pulled so tight it's as though it has never wanted to be released. Undoing intergenerational knot-work is slow and relentless and painful. Patience and resilience are required, and you need to accept that you might not be able to undo all of the knots in your lifetime.

There are moments in our lives when our parents tell us stories and we can feel their words being spoken into our bones, calling the past and shaping our future. Years ago, when Dad first told me the story of what happened to Uncle Eddie, I could feel the accordion of time stretching and compressing all at once. A wounded history shifted its presence to the here and now. Dad's voice was broken, suffocated. When he did speak, it was like a thundercloud that wanted to crack open and never stop raining. He shared the story carefully, slowly, not wanting to miss any details. Since the first time, Dad has shared the same story again and again. Over the years I've seen how Dad has carried this with him in his chest, in his eyes and across his back. Sometimes he gets what's called 'frozen shoulder'. As do I. It's the knot that we carry.

The story can begin differently depending on the moment. But it always ends like this: at 6.59pm on 18 August 1955, at the age of twenty, Edward Thomas Te Whiu was executed at Mt Eden Prison, Auckland, New Zealand.

~

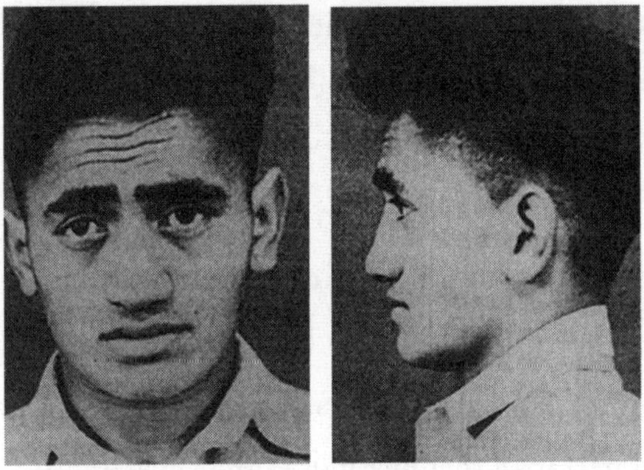

Edward Thomas Te Whiu

In researching and writing this piece, that sense of being frozen by mamae has been transmitted throughout my whole body. At times, grief and responsibility and fear and ineptitude have been overwhelming. Who am I to write this? My inner voice of self-reassurance says, *This is one of many beginnings – the undoing of another knot in the rope*. I recall the lifetime of anguish that Dad has embodied. I think of the steps Dad took to reclaim our whānau name. Dad's heart breaks again and again, remembering what happened to Eddie. I gently let Dad know that the act of writing these words is an act of undoing one of the knots in this tightly bound story.

Eddie's only remaining living sibling is Aunty Marion, the strongest aunty in the world. When the borders open and it's safe to travel to Auckland, I will spend slow time with Aunty Marion and sit with her and listen deeply. This story is a living document, and one that will change in time as experiences and people read and write in and out of it. For now, it's a place to start, pushing our waka away from the shoreline.

It has been frustrating and very predictable not to have been able to find any Māori voices in articles, newspapers or history books writing about Eddie's case. From my years of research, his too-short life has only been recorded through Pākehā lenses – lawyers, policemen and journalists who had a bias towards a narrative that justified Eddie's execution. The Eddie that I have heard my dad speak about is someone who was ultimately a survivor – someone born into a world where systems, support mechanisms, opportunities and the idea of living a 'good life' were not possible. Their accounts and opinions have compelled me to return to the page, no matter how difficult it is.

Perhaps the most recognised piece that has been composed about Eddie is a poem that the highly problematic yet renowned James K Baxter wrote in 1956, titled 'A Rope for Harry Fat'. Questions around permission obviously did not confront Baxter in '56. The privilege that comes with lack of connection and accountability is clear in the chasm between the way Baxter wrote and the enormous weight of responsibility we whānau feel in articulating another side to Eddie's story.

'He [Baxter] developed an interest in Māori culture, seeing Māori as marginalised and persecuted by mainstream society.' It is this privilege, which Baxter embodied, that enabled, empowered and encouraged him to write this poem and publish it without any hesitation. Did he think to contact Eddie's whānau for permission to share this work? Did he pause to consider that perhaps it wasn't his place to write such a poem? I doubt this very much. What's also troubling is that the public of New Zealand loved this poem, even referring to it as one of Baxter's 'finest'. I don't know if this poem is a 'fine' poem or not, but what I do know is that Baxter felt it was possible, permissible and passable to write about Eddie's death without flinching.

Sitting on the left of the page is Baxter's poem 'A Rope for Harry Fat' and opposite is my erasure poem, a revision piece that I constructed as a way of talking back to not only Baxter, but the system that allowed Eddie's execution to happen.

A Rope For Harry Fat	**Mauri Ora**
Oh some have killed in angry love	
And some have killed in hate,	
And some have killed in foreign lands	
To serve the business state.	
The hangman's hands are abstract hands	

Though sudden death they bring—	u
'The hangman keeps our country pure,'	
Says Harry Fat the king.	
Young love will kick the chairs about	
And like a rush fire burn,	
Desiring what it cannot have,	
A true love in return.	
Who knows what rage and darkness fall	n
When lovers' thoughts grow cold?	
'Whoever kills must pay the price,'	
Says Harry Fat the old.	
With violent hands a young man tried	d
To mend the shape of life.	
This one used a shotgun	
And that one used a knife.	
And who can see our issues plain	
That vex our groaning dust?	
'The law is greater than the man,'	
Says Harry Fat the just.	
Te Whiu was too young to vote,	
The prison records show.	

Some thought he was too young	o
to hang;	
Legality said No.	
Who knows what fear the	
raupo [sic] hides	
Or where the wild duck flies?	
'A trapdoor and a rope is best,'	
Says Harry Fat the wise.	
Though many a time he rolled his	
coat	
And on the bare boards lay,	
He lies in heavy concrete now	
Until the Reckoning Day.	
In linen sheet or granite aisle	t
Sleep Ministers of State.	
'We cannot help the idle poor,'	
Says Harry Fat the great.	
Mercy stirred like a summer wind	
The wigs and polished boots	h
And the long Jehovah faces	
Above their Sunday suits.	
The jury was uncertain;	
The judge debated long.	
'Let justice take her natural	
course,'	

Said Harry Fat the strong.

The butcher boy and the baker boy
Were whistling in the street
When the hangman bound Te Whiu's eyes
And strapped his hands and feet,
Who stole to buy a bicycle
And killed in panic blood.
'The parson won his soul at length,'
Said Harry Fat the good.

Oh some will kill in rage and fear
And some will kill in hate.
And some will kill in foreign lands
To serve the master State.
Justice walks heavy in the land,
She bears a rope and shroud.
'We will not change our policy,'
Says Harry Fat the proud.

e

k

n

o

t

Like prisons, archival institutions are highly controlled, powerful utilities of colonialism. They are built to hold bodies of information in, not let them out, no matter how miniscule or inconsequential they are. By their very design, national archives restrict those without a swipe card from multiple levels of multiple histories.

With several weeks of planning, providing every necessary form and proof of ID, and confirming my purpose for entry, I was given permission to spend an allocated amount of time reading the only file I was granted access to in Archives New Zealand. I was in Wellington, studying a Māori and Pasifika paper at the International Institute of Modern Letters, Victoria University. After many emails and phone calls, I finally received permission, so one day, as soon as class finished, I made my way to the Archives. It was a sunny afternoon. Once I was inside, the light immediately shifted as the once-was-blue-now-grey carpet set the mood. The chairs were grey plastic and the walls were off-white gone wrong. It felt like an emergency waiting room without a doctor in sight. This was where Eddie's files had been locked up tight for sixty-six years. This was the one file I was given access to. Inside were eight pages that were like tissue paper to hold. Despite living a life of twenty years, his file was paper thin.

EXTRACT: NGĀ TAONGA NZ SPECTRUM 415.

Leonard Poulter Leary, QC – Edward Te Whiu's lawyer
Interviewed by Jack Perkins from Radio NZ, 1982.

LPL: That is the whole basis of our great system of justice. It is the one contribution that poor old England has really made to the world. It's the principle that a man who is accused must be proved guilty.

JP: There was one particularly poignant case; it occurred in the '50s. The case of Te Whiu, the young Māori lad.

LPL: Yes.

JP: And he was hanged.

LPL: Yes, that's right.

JP: One of the last people I think to be hanged in New Zealand.

LPL: Yes, he was the second-to-last.

JP: Now that was a case that you defended. And lost.

LPL: Yes. Well, of course I felt very badly about him. I had tried the defence of 'Atavistic Fury' and it didn't go down, and it didn't deserve to go down. I don't think it was really sound.

JP: There was no question about whether the lad had murdered the old lady.

LPL: Oh, it was a brutal murder alright. He smashed her face to a pulp more or less, with his fist. And then poached himself some eggs and forged her signature after it. It didn't look like a mental aberration, did it? On the other hand, he was a very likeable boy. That's the extraordinary thing, that lots of people who do dreadful things seem perfectly normal. I liked Te Whiu. I felt very sorry for him. And although I couldn't see I could've done very much …

JP: Why did you feel sorry for him? For a brutal murderer?

LPL: Well because I'd felt that he'd had a bad run. He was chased all round the country, a sort of fugitive, hunted off a farm and so on and cold and miserable and hiding. At a time when what principles you may have sink into the background and you want food and shelter, and this is the way he took it.

JP: This is what brought him to the old lady's house.

LPL: Breaking in to the house and killing the old lady, whom he knew. And if he'd asked her, I expect she would have fed him and housed him. At any rate I felt that there was a touch of the 'Atavistic Fury' about it.

JP: Now, what do you mean by 'Atavistic Fury'?

LPL:

He dropped back to the

S A V A G E

M Ā O R I that

he'd only BEEN

two generations

before. His forebears

would've thought nothing

of the incident.

JP: You have a certain theory about this, don't you?

LPL: I think it's safe to say that nine men out of ten that commit an offence have just some little weaknesses that events have played on, caught them out. Any one of us might have committed an offence. In fact, I would go so far as to say, 'Let him who is without sin cast the first stone'.

LPL: Well, I went to see Te Whiu – the head of the jail went with me – and we went through clanging doors and long, long depressing passages, and we came to the 'Condemned Cell' – they've got one that they called the Condemned Cell at that time – and when I arrived two priests came out and I went in. And I was … I didn't quite know how to … err … pass my word of condolence – take the blame on myself for what had happened. Gosh, he was going to be hanged in half an hour.

JP: Now what did the inside of that cell look like?

LPL: Oh well, it was stuffy, there was some light from high up. And on the couch was his untasted breakfast, I suppose, or bits of it. There was a dirty plate and there were all sorts of pathetic little things around on the couch. He'd written the names on them of his family, he wanted them to have them. I took this all in quickly and drew a breath and was going to wish him more luck in the next world than he'd had in this one, I suppose, when he lifted up his hand and said, 'God bless you, Mr Leary, thank you for all you've done.' Well, of course that just broke me up. And I left on that note. And a little bit later on as I was moping over the hill to Mt Eden, I think is the little township, and I looked at my watch and I knew that it was twenty minutes after my interview, and Te Whiu was no more.

It was Leonard Poulter Leary's last comment that brought a flood of fire-filled tears when I first heard this interview. Later, words from a brilliant speech for JustSpeak by Moana Jackson, Ngāti Kahungunu and Ngāti Porou lawyer, provided salve:

> And part of the dissidence I think in this country about calling things racist is that there has developed since 1840 this myth that colonisation and the dispossession of Māori people was somehow better than the dispossession of other Indigenous peoples. That the Crown was somehow honourable in its determination to take away our land, our lives and our power. But to have a notion of an 'honourable colonisation', or of an 'honourable dispossession' is fundamentally a contradiction in terms. You can't honourably dispossess someone of who they are, their lands, their language, their history and so on. But the creation of the idea of a 'better than somewhere else'

colonisation led to the idea that, as a result, race relations between Māori and others was better than anywhere else in the world. And so, if there were issues like prejudice or bias, say, in corrections policies and so on, they easily get sidelined as being aberrations, as being exceptions to the rule. And people do get uncomfortable talking about racism, but if we don't talk about racism, it's rather like if women didn't challenge the patriarchy by talking about sexism. It's as though women could challenge misogyny without naming it as sexism.

And we don't seem to have a difficulty with using the term 'sexism'. But we do seem to have a problem with using the comparative word, in a different sense: 'racism'. So, part of the necessary debate, part of the necessary conversation, leading towards the eventual abolition of prisons, in my view, is to be honest about how we frame that conversation. And to acknowledge the racism of colonisation, because in the end, colonisation was driven by decisions made in Europe that so-called white, civilised countries had a right to dispossess peoples who were not white and not 'civilised'. And although there were lots of other contributing factors to that dispossession, the mad economic drive for wealth and so on, the fundamental framework within which colonisation operated was a racist one. And it was from that racist framework that prisons and the subsequent development of corrections policies developed in this country.

The 1950s was the last decade in which capital punishment was practised in New Zealand. Of the twenty-eight men executed for murder in the 20th century, eight were hanged in the 1950s – four in 1955 alone. Among those executed that year was twenty-year-old Edward Te Whiu. Despite serious questions over his 'childlike mental state', Eddie was convicted in just thirty-five minutes for the murder of pensioner Florence Smith.

Mt Eden Prison, 1960s

I dwell in the in-between space. I bridge the Pacific, feet in Australia with arms outstretched to Aotearoa. The in-between places are where energy is woven in time and space, ancient swirling waters merge with skies from the future. When Eddie visits me, it is in these zones of stillness and ancient vibration. I use the word 'visit' because I don't know any other way to describe it. Maybe if I say, 'he comes to me', it might translate better? His energy is not that of a straight-up ghost and definitely not a monster or ghoul. He is neither light nor dark, his spirit does not seek revenge, instead, it feels like Eddie wants to be listened to. He's been in dreams that have woken me up. I'll look towards the doorway and feel his presence there. He doesn't scare me or cause me distress. His hauntings are reminders to keep writing and not forget him. Eve Tuck (Unangax̂ scholar) says that 'hauntings can be theories of change' and this resonates with so much clarity and reclamation. Having three brothers, two of whom have had schizophrenia since they were in their late teens, I've been very familiar with people experiencing 'voices'. This is not what it's like when Eddie connects with me. His wairua, his spirit, is that of a twenty-year-old frozen in time, seeking again and again to be understood, to know he is remembered, to know he lived life and to tell me, tell us, we must live.

Eddie's returnings are a quiet defiance, something I will not turn away from. Tuck goes on to say, 'Haunting doesn't hope to change people's perceptions, nor does it hope for reconciliation. Haunting lies precisely in its refusal to stop. Alien to settlers and generative to us ghosts, this refusal to stop is its own form of resolving. For ghosts, the haunting is the resolving, it is not what needs to be resolved. Haunting aims to wrong the wrongs, a confrontation that settler horror aims to evade.'

Eddie compels me to return to myself and to a place that is full of magnetic pull. Daily I go to the Hokianga in my mind – a place where the harbour holds ancient light and our whakapapa. I ride a time portal, returning again and again to Aotearoa, knowing that I am getting closer to living there one day. I can feel it in my bones.

BIGAN

Interlude

Nardi Simpson

giirrlayaay gigilaya
waal manumaldaya
waal murrunbaagu
yalagiirr dhiyamalday
giirrlayaay gigilaya

gayliyaay
with Priscilla Strasek Barker

bilba gayaay-dhi wuru-gi-la-nha. burrul nguungu manga
buyaduul nguungu dhurrun
giirr dhuniya-ga-nha baabi-la-nha
buluuy-dha-nha yana-waa-nha. gayaay-dhu bilba
ngarrangarra-lda-nha
maliyaa nhama.gaalay
yaama bilba-gu gayaay gundhi, dhaymaarr-u-bala bilba-gu
gundhi wuu-dha-nha?

garrii muyaan-da dhurra-lda-nha. guyayn buyabuya
gagan.gagan nguungu. giirr nhama guyayn baluwaa

burranbay-la-nha
muyaan-gu guyayn-du bayama-lda-nhi
muyaan banuwa-giirr
bamba gaali bayama-laa-nha wagi ngaarribaagili
yaama garrii-gu dhanduwi-y-la-y muyaan-gu, muyaan-gu-
bala dhanduwi-y-la-y garrii-dja?

dhaymaarr mulan buluuy. banuwa nhama
ngaaybu
mulamula nhama, man.gaman.ga-bula
murrunbaa guwaymbarra-bala
walanbaa
balal
murrila nhama
biyuurra-laa-ya nhama
banuwa-nginda gulbirr muyaan, dhii. murrila-nginda-bala
murrunbaa
wila-y-la-nha-gili ganugu
dhurra-li ganugu nguwa burrul gi-gi
yaama banuwa-ga dhilay-rraa-nha murrila-dhi, murrila-gu-
bala dhuwima-laa-nha
banuwa-gu?

wagi-dja banaga-waa-nha gaawaa

gayma-laa-nha, wirra-laa-nha nhama
ngandirr nguwagili, ngandirr ngaarrigili-bula
giirr nhama gaawaa gundhi-dja ngaaluurr, dhugaalubaa,
girrabirrii, gumaay, yin.ga, yuwayaa
dhanduwi-y-la-nha ganunga bidjaaybiyaay gali-dja
gali-dja. miimii-dja dhayn, dhii baabi-lda-nha
yaama gali-dju garra-laa-nha dhaymaarr, dhaymaarr-yu-bala
gali-dju dhama-la-nha?

gaawaa-ga baabi-lda-nha maangi
walanbaa nguungu waa
guuya-lda-nha nhama
banggabaa
ngulu-ga dhurra-laa-nha ngamulngamul
gali banaga-waa-nha-giirr
giirr nhama waa garran.garraan muwi-la-nha
yili-dja buuwiy-la-nha dhingaa
wirrunbiyaay
gunganbiyaay, mulamula
dhiyaagarra-ga buuwiy-la-nha, baliyaa, gayn.gayn
waa-ga guuma-y-la-nha mulamula
wadhagii
yaama dhingaa gugirriidhalibaa waa-gu-bala, dhingaa
yalaa-gu?

maa birralii-dju nguwa-laa-nha
wamu nguungu maa
maa nguungu gurru
gunagala-ga nguungu maa yuurrambi-la-nha
baluwaa
barraay-nga
ganaay muwi-la-nha-nga birralii-dju maa
winangay-la-nha nguungu
yaama birralii gaa-gi-la-nha, wuu-raa-nha-bala nguungu?

Kind

A bilby buries in the sand. Its ears are big. Its fur is short. It sleeps in the day. It moves at night. The sand is its protector. Bilby is its friend. Does Bilby own its sandy burrow or does land give Bilby a home?

An orchid grows from the hollow of a tree. The flower is thin. It is colourful. It blooms quietly. The flower attaches to the branch. The tree is its soil. They hold each other tight above the plains. Does orchid exist for tree or tree exist for orchid?

Part of the land is black. It is black soil. It is rich. It is soft and it is flat. The other is red. Hard. Dry. It is ridge. It rolls. Some trees and creatures want black soil. Others need red sand. Each stay to their side. Where they flourish and grow. Does black dirt push at red sand or red rock dominate soil?

A river turns through the plain. It bends and twists. A steep bank on either side. The water is the home of fish, shrimp, turtle, water rat, yabby, frog. They live in its muddy flow. Life appears at its edges and within the water's flow. Does water divide land or cradle its touch?

A mussel sleeps in the riverbed. Its shell is hard. It shines. White. Ripples appear on its surface. Like the flow of the water around it. Shell closes tight. Between its lips rests meat. Succulent. Juicy and soft. Resting upon a cold, smooth bed. Shell hides this softness. A secret. Is meat shell's weakness or is shell meat's captor?

Baby makes a fist. Her fingers are fat. Her palm is round. Her hand waves in the air. Slow. Then fast. Baby's hands open then close. She is learning. Does baby take or does she give?

** illustration by gunugayngaa ngay (my sister's daughter), Hawaiiki Te Peeti*

I AM ...

L-FRESH The LION

One of my favourite paintings is of a Nihang Singh sitting cross-legged overlooking a farm. I remember the first time I saw it. The deep royal blue of his baana and the lush green fields attracted my attention to this moment in time. He is an elderly Nihang. His strong, white and flowing beard comes midway down his chest, exuding wisdom from a life having been lived. He looks relaxed. I assume content too, gazing upon his crops as if he is gracefully and gratefully recalling memories, as I imagine one does as they approach their final days. He, no doubt, has stories to tell. What made this painting even more memorable to me was the caption that accompanied it:

> I was a soldier so my son could be a farmer.
> And my son was a farmer so that his son could be a poet.

The painting takes on a new meaning. This inspiring Nihang warrior isn't overseeing his own farm but that of his son. I have so many questions running through my mind. *How many battles had he fought? What time period was he from* (so I could get a sense of the imagined or real historical context)? *What was his name? What was his son's name? Where in Panjab are they from? And who painted this scene? Was it his grandson?*

It makes me think of my grandparents with a sense of gratitude and fondness. A glowing warmth in my chest and a smile prompts a memory of my nani ji sitting in her favourite chair with my nana ji at her side. Both of them surrounded by my parents and extensive collection of aunties, uncles and cousins in the way a family usually gathers comfortably around a TV during the Boxing Day Test Match. Her welcoming laughter encourages a gentle softness on the face of my nana ji. Nana ji and nani ji. It was my mother's parents who made the long migration journey from Jagraon in Panjab to Glenfield in South-West Sydney, Australia. They left behind not only a very successful timber and furniture business but also their family and friends. And whether they were conscious of it or not, they also left behind the unspoken comfort and safety that comes with living in your motherland: being in a place where the Sikh way of life was and still is cultivated without interruption (for the most part). They no longer had proximity to countless historical sites – treasure troves of inspiration. They left behind the history and legacy of not just our entire community, but, as I would come to learn later in life, also of our family. They traded that for a distant land with a confusing foreign language they now had to learn, and for a developing suburb with zero social and community support networks. They came to reside in a place they couldn't relate to culturally. A place that viewed them as strange, exotic, backwards and sometimes dangerous and unintelligent. They moved to a place that perceived them as lesser, their culture and language as funny and inferior, and the colour of their skin as 'diverse'.

If they were aware of that context of mid-'80s Australia and what it meant for them, they never showed it. I can't ever recall seeing my grandparents sad, frustrated, burned out or defeated. They were the opposite of that, always smiling, optimistic and beaming with an energy that was both life-giving and magnetic. I say magnetic because they went from knowing no one (having followed their eldest child and her husband to Australia) to their humble home in Glenfield, becoming a community hub for Sikhs and Panjabis from across the entire South-West Sydney region. From having no support to becoming a support for the community. On any given day of the week there was always a community aunty or uncle popping in with their young kids, on top of my own big family of four aunties and two uncles – most married and with multiple kids of their own. The front door was hardly ever locked. Their home was a hub, for real. They dedicated so much of their time to family and to our community. They volunteered at the local emerging Gurdwaras religiously, helping to establish them as safe community spaces. I have so many warm memories of my nani ji, my mum and my aunties cooking in Gurdwara kitchens or in their own home kitchens or over portable gas burners in the garage for Sikh community paath and kirtan programs. I can recall their laughs spreading and embracing everybody in close proximity, welcoming more hands and laughs into the kitchen.

I think of my grandparents and my parents as the farmers, both metaphorically and literally. My nani ji's Glenfield backyard resembled a community plot of vegetables nestled between two homes in a pind. Countless greens for her saag, okra for the sabzi, and strawberries for the poorly dug trapping pits that my cousins and I would set up to catch my mamma ji's home visiting nurse, Craig. My mamma ji was seriously injured in a car crash leaving him with physical and mental disabilities. He required full-time care, provided by my grandparents and shared between my mother and aunties, for the rest of his life. I was too young to remember the accident that changed his life and the lives of everybody in our family. When I ask my mum about that time, she recalls in a softer voice the conversations with doctors who said her brother would never be able to walk again. She remembers the constant prayers and the moment of defiant triumph when my mamma ji would go on to prove doctors wrong by standing on his two feet and taking his first steps post-accident. Of all the cricket fans in my extended family, there is none greater than my mamma ji. During the summers when India played against Australia, the entire family would sit around the TV. All of us cheering on India except for my mamma ji, whose unwavering loyalty to the Australian cricket team, despite the rest of us sledging him, signified to me his deep gratitude for his adopted country.

My nani ji produced her own homemade compost in an upside-down black bin that us kids used as a makeshift wicket in our highly competitive backyard cricket matches. She also had a mango tree in the front yard, which only ever blessed us with one fruit. Once my nani ji saw it, she took extra care of the tree that was giving birth to this gift. She watched it day by day and her excitement grew as the baby mango grew. She would converse with the tree, showering it with positive affirmations while feeding it with the garden hose. She didn't actually lean over and kiss the tree in the way a grandmother does her beloved grandchildren, but that's the image that comes to mind when I recall her loving and caring for it. Her excitement over harvesting her first mango continued to grow, until one morning a passer-by took it from the tree, a thief in the night, leaving my nani ji in tears when she realised she had been robbed. I've never seen anyone as passionate about their crops as her. A farmer through-and-through, from the pind to the burbs. Just like my father.

Our Glenfield backyard is surely one of a kind. Pumpkin vines on the left with the herbs, tomatoes, chilli trees, spinach and okra. Lemons and oranges along the back fence with the kale, eggplant and capsicums; and sweet potato, carrots, garlic and karela near the row of sugar cane along the right-side fence. Yes, sugar cane in Glenfield. It is my father's favourite. Don't ask him how he did it, he just did. His sugar cane produces enough raw cane to chew, juice and boil down into gur for my entire extended family and then some. It's a scene, for real, come sugar-cane harvest season: my dad chopping them down with his machete, me and my brother taking turns to carry them to the garage where they are fed through a home-rigged sugar-cane juicer run by an old garage-door motor. The machine squeezes the juice out into a steel bowl, some of which goes into jugs or glass bottles and then straight into the fridge. The rest goes directly into Mum's big pot, which rests on top of the same garage gas burner that we all used to sit around in my grandparents' makeshift kitchen, starting the process of making the gur that will end up in our cups of cha or hot milk.

Then there's the scene that ties it all together for me: seeing my dad sitting on a wooden outdoor chair, wrapped in a characteristically Panjabi shawl as if being embraced and protected from the morning cold by generations of Sikh ancestors. Machete in one hand and sugar cane in the other. Chopping the cane, chewing it and spitting out the remains – all the while overseeing his version of the village farm, like the Nihang Singh in the painting. When I see him back there, I find myself wondering what he's thinking about as he chops and chews away. Is he reminiscing about his rangla Panjab, where as a child he and his friends would chase after the tractors bearing sugar cane stacked layer-upon-layer in a pyramid, the ends hanging off the trailer like an oversized hand-me-down hoodie? Does he imagine trying to grab a cane off the back while dodging the long, flailing stick of the guard sitting on top of the pyramid? I remember my dad describing that memory to me. At the time we were in Panjab, standing on the side of the road at a pitstop where trucks would load or unload their cargo, which was mostly fresh produce. Our taxi had a flat tyre and we were waiting for the driver's contact to drop off a spare. The sun was setting as we waited, and approaching us on the road was a slowly moving pyramid of sugar cane. We both laughed when some kids ran up to the trailer, evading the swipes from the resolute sugar-cane defender's long stick.

My family dedicated their lives to planting seeds so I guess it was only right that I became their poet, their storyteller.

It's only because of their journey, their never-tired-in-the-face-of-hardship mindset, their unshakeable discipline to remain firm in their faith, culture and their self-made village in Australia, that I was able to become a songwriter and an artist. I may not have walked in their shoes, but I carry the stories they never got the opportunity to tell. They were too busy building a foundation that would allow my younger brother and I to be brave, bold, ambitious and creative.

Every time I write, I'm aware of what it took to get here. Every song is purposeful. Every bar is fiercely passionate and every word carries weight. Nothing goes to waste, just like in my nani ji's garden. Spoken like a true farmer's son. I have to tell their stories because if I don't, then who will?

This is a collection of stories. Our stories:

The son of two migrants
Who hoped that their kid would shine brightest
But where we come from it's a rough climate
Still I rose to become one of the South West's finest
In this game they gave us snakes but we climbers
Life's all good if you're acing your assignments
The stars ain't ever in alignment
But if there's a way then we got the will to find it
Move with the times but my goal to be timeless

Inspired by the grind and the whole scene's vibrance
Community teaches you humility and kindness
When one of us wins the feeling is priceless
The odds stacked against us, when you open your eyelids
You learn quick, discrimination's a virus
They try paint us with one brush and simplify us
But their labels don't define us
Survival mindset can sometimes produce a blindness
To the struggles of the land we on, caught up in silence
Remember the times when, we left for this island—
Continent, oppression and pain in our consciousness
When we arrived our skills weren't recognised
From your eyes your parents' work ethic never dies
You inherit their dreams coz they never got the chance
Too busy building things with their bare hands
But that's pressure, especially when your vision is extra
That takes next-level effort, and you trying to be the best that
You can be, despite the negativity
You're not prepared for a fight but they paint you as the enemy
Stealing their jobs when you want equal treatment
Complaining non-stop, that's what they say when you speak up
Be grateful is what they try teach us
Not knowing that for everything we have we had to reach up
And grab it, work hard, establish new habits

Some rise to the challenge, some fall trying to manage
The expectation, excuse my hesitation
To celebrate a nation that barely appreciates us
That won't face its demons in the name of healing
Who built a foundation off of pillaging and stealing?
And will it ever change? ਮੈਨੂੰ ਨਹੀਂ ਪਤਾ
They may never understand us, (what?) I didn't stutter
We from the West

This life is a gift, man. For me specifically, being born into a Sikh family and inheriting such a rich, inspiring legacy is something I have taken for granted, for real. If I said that it wouldn't bother me if I lost my family and friends, my home and my studio, my business, my favourite kicks or any of the material things that bring me comfort so long as I still had the Guru's Sikhi, I'd be bullshitting. I know I don't fully understand or appreciate its value.

There's a very high standard set in the pages and oral stories of Sikh history. There are many examples of great Sikhs who dedicated themselves to this path. With the blessings of the Guru, they centred their lives around an unwavering discipline in their spiritual practice. Their contribution to the world, how they uplifted, supported, protected, liberated and empowered communities, is unrivalled. So is the way they battled against the odds (metaphorically and literally), taking on oppressive regimes to push the values of equality and sovereignty. I grew up hearing these types of stories, told by my family or by Sants, kirtanis and katha vachaks at the local Gurdwaras scattered across Sydney. Forty Sikhs versus an army of one million, all of them ready to run into the arms of death, unafraid and without hesitation, with a true chardi kala spirit: this, the Battle of Chamkaur, is one of the stories I inherited at birth.

Whenever we had the chance to fly to Panjab as a family, my parents made certain we visited the places where such stories took place. From Sri Kesgarh Sahib in Anandpur Sahib, where five Sikhs gave their heads to the tenth Guru at the first Amrit Sanchar ceremony in 1699 (and where I would, hundreds of years later, undergo the same ceremony at twenty-six years old), to Sri Harmandir Sahib in Amritsar, where there are endless stories of victory and sacrifice in overthrowing tyranny and acts of seva. We walked where great Sikh leaders led a small army to successfully reclaim Sri Harmandir Sahib for our people. The same place where, on the 1984 anniversary of the shaheedi of the fifth Guru, a revered Sant and a small collective of brave Sikhs held off the Indian Army's assault operation for seven days despite encountering heavily armed ground troops and tanks. We saw where the fourth Guru brought peace and many invaluable teachings to congregations of people who travelled from all corners of the region to visit the blessed sarovar of Amritsar.

We'd also travel to lesser-known historically significant places that my parents mostly found through word of mouth within our community. I remember being in taxis, driving along dirt roads that bordered lush green fields of village farms in Panjab where wild peacocks would jump over the path just ahead of us, annoyed that us outsiders had disturbed their usual peace. We would arrive at a small village Gurdwara. There, we'd be welcomed by a pointed white-marble dome and yellow Khalsa flag, breaking the long stretch of green fields that us Panjabis across the globe love and celebrate. My mum would giggle like an excited child. My dad would say, 'ਅਸ ਪਹੁੰਚ ਗਏ.' I'd ask them to remind me of the history of the place, trying to picture the scenes as our taxi pulled up to the patch of dirt and rubble that was the designated car park. There would be fewer than a handful of people there doing seva (the act of serving without expecting or even thinking of receiving any recognition, commendation or benefit in return), taking care of the Gurdwara and looking after any arrivals. The sevadars would welcome us with great enthusiasm and be surprised to learn we had travelled from Australia. They'd gift us all-access guided tours, giving detailed recounts of the historical events that took place at that location, narrated so beautifully and poetically in our mother tongue. The aesthetic was fulfilling for me despite having to ask my parents to translate the parts I couldn't quite catch or understand.

In some locations, we would also get to see sacred artefacts from the stories we'd all heard since reciting Mool Mantar for our grandparents and their friends. Like at one location in Anandpur Sahib, where we met the direct descendants of the sevadars entrusted with caretaking duties by the tenth Guru. The artefacts kept there belonged to the Guru. The caretakers showed us a battle-torn chola he wore along with a small handwritten pothi that Guru Sahib used to keep in his dastaar and the tag he used to tie to the foot of his baaz. This bird is so iconic that every baaz almost serves as a symbol for the Guru's presence. When Sikhs across the globe saw photographs of a baaz present during key moments of the 2020–21 farmers' protest in Delhi, we all collectively felt uplifted, sensing the protection of the Khalsa Panth's father.

At another small Gurdwara, this time on the side of a highway near a dusty village market, we saw two large brass cups. They were used by the tenth Guru's two youngest sons when they were held prisoner in the tund burj with their grandmother before being brutally executed for refusing to renounce their Sikhi, their father and their sovereignty. When asked what they would do if they were released, they said they'd follow in the footsteps of their father by gathering the Khalsa Army to challenge oppression wherever it stands, that they'd overthrow the Mughal Empire. They were entombed alive, bricked into the wall at ages six and nine, suffocating until the wall collapsed just before their last breath, and their throats were slit. Not once were they afraid. They embraced this opportunity to give shaheedi. Now their stories are told to every Sikh child around the globe.

Seeing these places and sacred artefacts over various trips to India and Panjab has grounded me. With each visit I gathered new stories from our history. I came home inspired to learn more, and feeling less alone. Now that I've reclaimed my mother tongue, the trips mean even more to me. I feel a sense of belonging in Panjab. This belonging is effortless compared to the exhausting experience of trying to force a sense of belonging in Australia – which is like trying to jam that single puzzle piece into a spot where it doesn't fit. Each trip to Panjab solidified my theory that my belonging (there and here) isn't dependent upon the pieces and how they fit around me. Instead, my sense of belonging is in knowing that I am who I am. Those trips have instilled within me a now unshakeable resilience, a defiant strength and a persistent faith.

But it hasn't always been this way. The end of primary school and my years in high school had me divided and uncertain about my identity and my place in Australia. At school, I never backed down or withheld from fighting back against bullies, even if I was outnumbered or outsized. I was a skinny brown boy but I had more than my weight in staunch determination. Whether it was in facing the racial sledges of my primary school classmates during sport or challenging a high school teacher who demanded that my brother 'take his hat off' (referring to his patka) in front of his entire class, I made sure to stand my ground and let it be known that I wasn't going to let it fly.

My brother, younger than me by four years, enrolled at my high school after a few years at a neighbouring school in the area. I've always been protective of my brother. During one recess break, I saw him in the quad where my classmates and I would usually hang out. I asked how he was doing and he told me that one of his teachers had racially abused him in front of the entire class after he had been caught chewing gum. I was fuming. I went straight to the teacher, who happened to be walking nearby, and confronted him. I told him what he said wasn't okay and that he owed my brother an apology. He refused, failing to see why what he had said was an issue. I raised it with the school to the point where a formal complaint was made and a mediation session was arranged between myself, my brother, the teacher who had made the racist comment, one of my teachers (who attended to support us) and the principal. I remember being reduced to tears the moment I realised there would be no consequences for the teacher. Instead, we got the standard, 'I'm sorry if you were offended,' coupled with the teacher telling us that he'd been a supporter of Indigenous rights movements in the past. As the tears slowly rolled down my cheeks, all I could think was that I'd failed in my duty to protect my brother.

It's experiences like these that fuel my drive make music that serves a purpose, to make music with a message:

> My parents named me Sukhdeep, it means to be a light for peace
> Born with a purpose, it took a while for me to find my feet
> A nervous child in the wild where they're eyeing my defeat
> But now they pay attention whenever they hear The LION speak
> I don't play no games, this ain't no hide and seek
> Aware of my position, born into a dying breed
> Surrounded by fallacy, deception and apathy
> First-world ego and civilised savagery
> I turn on the news but there's nothing new to me
> Losing brain cells debating those who speak stupidly
> Developed hard skin so I'm immune to the scrutiny

My survival lessons were infused with turmeric and some cumin seeds
Nothing can break me, nothing can shake me
My roots are real deep so the wind can never take me
But it wasn't always like that, it took many years
Before I realised I had what I needed right here
Here, listen to my heart speak
I won't let this moment pass me
I close my eyes and pay fine attention
It's time for greatness, no excuses, no exceptions
Forever rising, I was made for ascension
To carry on through the storm with unparalleled effort
To share my inner truths through this musical expression
In the booth, on my records, with the name I was blessed with
May you forgive the mistakes I made on this album
Over a lifetime we collect them in the thousands
May my family, friends and fans keep me grounded
I hope no matter what that I never let 'em down and
May the blessings never end, may I catch 'em when they descend
And keep it 100 and never be one to pretend
May there be many more songs for me to bring to life
May I live to be great with my purpose clear in sight
To be Peace and Light

I need to point out that to bemoan being a minority or to view it as a negative is not a concept that is ever expressed in Sikhi. If anything, our community is taught via countless examples in our history that quality is key. We don't ever fear being outnumbered. We don't see a lack of numbers as an obstacle. Sikhs visibly stand out. We are meant to. Our Gurus made us that way. But for me, as a kid in South-West Sydney, living in a country that knew very little about my community and had zero understanding of our history, culture, practices, language and visible identity meant that none of these were valued or accepted.

I don't know what people thought seeing a short, skinny young brown boy with his hair in a topknot, wrapped tightly in green fabric to match his school uniform. But I do know what it felt like to constantly attract often awkward and sometimes aggressive stares and comments. I became hyper-alert, always aware of my surroundings, how many people were around and how many of them were staring, laughing or mocking me.

I even developed a suspicion of my friends because some of them ignorantly took aim at my difference. I remember one time after school, being picked up by my dad in our bottle-green Toyota Camry. Without asking my dad first, I'd offered two of my friends a ride to the train station as it was on our way home. My dad had a burned MP3 CD of kirtan, Sikh worship music, playing in the car. The sounds of the harmonium playing in raag while a tabla kept the beat and the sweet-sounding vocalist singing Gurbani must have, no doubt, reminded my dad of his Panjab. Now something I regard as the highest form of music was, back then, a source of regrettable shame for me, as my two friends quietly joked and laughed at this foreign music. It made me feel like it was inferior, and that by listening to it, I must be inferior too. So, there I was, divided. A part of me had proudly inherited the Sikh warrior spirit and the social justice values, while the other part wanted to run away from all the things that highlighted my difference to the world.

Looking back, I don't blame my friends. We are all products of our environment. Ours, especially at that time, encouraged assimilation in such a toxic way that in order to fit in or be 'normal', making fun of others' differences had become like a rite of passage. We couldn't be accepted if we didn't dish it out at some point. There was no thinking of what that meant for the person on the receiving end. There was no awareness of mental health and wellbeing. This was the era where the best the country could be expected to do was to 'tolerate' cultural and racial differences. Tolerate.

By age thirteen, I had developed what I'd later come to know as anxiety, experiencing regular panic attacks that impacted my relationship with food. Until my mid-to-late twenties,

I struggled to eat in public places, even in the company of family or close friends, and especially with unfamiliar people. If I had a show, I couldn't eat for the whole day. By the end, I'd be so exhausted that when I slept, I'd be awoken by fits of dry heaving and vomiting. It's something I no longer experience, having put in a lot of work to understand, overcome and come to peace with my journey. But back then, for all those years, I would desperately wish for a life without this anxiety. I'd keep telling myself, *Man, if this is what I can do while experiencing this shit, imagine what I could do without it.* Now I realise that I wouldn't be who I am without having gone through those experiences and learning to go inside to understand myself.

The cost of me navigating this internal division, the warzone, the conflict between cultures, was too great. And the most significant casualty in this war was the loss of my mother language, Panjabi:

> You ever seen a world die?
> It's happening before our very eyes
> Nothing is sacred even the tongue gets gentrified
> Shame is a colloquialism of genocide
> Remember when for speaking mother tongue people got
> penalised
> Legacy and tradition elders have memorised

Ain't cool enough for kids these days to recognise
Motherland, Mother Tongue, a man can fantasise
Hold on, may the culture be strong, Aquemini
Whispered in the shadow of oppression to survive
A heavy price was paid, the cost was their lives
Now we dumb it down, centuries simplified
If we had another chance would we press rewind
My pride too real, it rarely gets televised
A burden is a blessing, a lesson that's set aside
Speaking to the next generation I emphasise
For you to carry the weight, you need to exercise
Your Mother Tongue
I don't want to lose you
Coz you mean too much
I said you mean too much
Conversations with my grandmother would comfort me
I'd reply in our mother tongue uncomfortably
She'd laugh, unaware of the shame kept underneath
The process of losing it wasn't done consciously
My language, words I spoke so beautifully
There was kids' competitions held by the community
I got pictures standing on podiums that you should see
Fast-forward five years and lost my fluency
I remember back when I was kicking it in school

At that age speaking ya language wasn't cool
If you stood out they'd make you feel like a fool
The pressure from your peers is very powerful
Now it's a slow journey, I'm just trying to relearn
Hoping that one day the spirit of it returns
The ancestors reaching, they just want to be heard
Cherish the vocab, grateful for each word
My Mother Tongue

'Changes' by Tupac Shakur changed the game for me. By age fourteen I had immersed myself in hip-hop music. When I found 2Pac, I became obsessed with his music. I watched all of the 2Pac documentaries and explored all the conspiracy theories about his death (or fake death, depending on who you ask). I immaturely identified with his Thug Life movement. Though I was never gang affiliated, the theme of the underdog taking on an entire system that counted him out resonated with me. I hunted through physical and online urbanwear stores to find any of 2Pac's Makaveli brand clothes, copping myself a few pairs of baggy jeans and a massively oversized hoodie just so I could rock something 2Pac-related. Everyone could see the obsession. I didn't hide it.

In Year 10 I did a school presentation about 2Pac's mother, Afeni, and the Black Panther Party (BPP). In studying for that presentation, I learned about the civil rights movement in the United States and the influence it has had on so many of my favourite hip-hop artists. In my speech, I shared examples of how the BPP would look after African–American communities by providing free breakfast to children before school as well as free education to underprivileged kids. I had photographs of BPP founders Huey P Newton and Bobby Seale on one slide, then 2Pac's song 'Trapped' playing on the next. I remember my mum gifting me his *Better Dayz* album for one of my birthdays, which I'd repeatedly play on our family stereo in the TV room (probably one of the very few non-kirtan CDs that got played on that stereo). I remember my friends from Year 12 music class getting me a framed copy of the *Resurrection* movie poster for my birthday too.

2Pac's work resonated with me deeply. He was passionate about social justice and the principles of freedom, sovereignty, self-determination and empowerment. He spoke for his community and fearlessly expressed their struggles in his music. I couldn't relate to his specific experience of being a young African–American male from the ghetto, but I definitely related to his feelings of being marginalised and voiceless. I also resonated with his warrior spirit, which felt very familiar to me as a young Sikh boy who grew up on the countless stories of Sikh warriors. His music helped me tap into and discover things within me that I had no idea of how to understand or explain. Internally, I was making the connections between my experiences and learning to unpack and understand my relationship with that legacy of Sikhi that I inherited at birth.

At that point in my life, same as now, my parents strongly encouraged me to develop a connection with Sikhi. But we know how teenagers are – they don't listen. They have to do things their own way. In the absence of Sikh role models in the media I was engaging with, namely music, hearing 2Pac proudly rap about his roots and standing up for his community made this young Sikh boy feel like it was cool to own where you're from. So, I started researching online, reading books and listening more carefully whenever my parents or grandparents shared Sikh stories in our home. I became less *influenced* by 2Pac and more *inspired* by him – inspired to learn more about myself and what makes me unique.

When I started getting known for releasing music and performing publicly, I would field questions from Australian music and entertainment media as well as Panjabi and Sikh media asking why I chose hip-hop. I think what they were trying to say, in a diplomatic way, was why was this Sikh kid making rap music and not working at a 7-Eleven or driving a taxi or studying to become a doctor, engineer or lawyer? To be fair, I did study law and arts like a good desi son, but that's beside the point. The connection between a young Sikh from

Western Sydney and hip-hop may not have made sense to people from the outside looking in, but to me it is harmony. Whenever I was asked about it, I tried to explain this feeling of harmony, but the more I tried to simplify my experience and make hip-hop and Sikhi sound similar to each other, the more unsettling it felt. There are similarities in their values of social justice, empowerment, self-determination, knowledge and community just to name a few, but the contexts that birthed them and the expressions that come from each are very different. As such, they can't be compared. It ain't a simple black and white. There are many shades of grey.

To me, to try and be a Sikh means to humble yourself, to offer your head to the Guru and to use your hands in service of the Guru's principles, values and teachings. It means putting your ego aside to recognise that your achievements in this lifetime aren't your own. They're a blessing. And they can't compare to the legacies left by the many great Sikhs who came before. What is an ARIA nomination in comparison to dedicating your entire life to singing the Guru's bani with an undying love and unwavering focus as a Sikh musician? How can it compare to continuing to sing from the depths of your heart and soul without hesitation, even when the stage becomes a raging battlefield of thunder-striking sword clashes or a hailstorm of bullets and bombs, because the thought of abandoning your service to the Guru is a pain worse than death? There is no comparison.

To me, hip-hop is a way of thinking, speaking and behaving. It's a code, an influencer of culture and a ripple in the ocean that continues to spread, making waves and reaching shores across the globe. In hip-hop, creativity is valued and celebrated at a group and individual level. Through hip-hop, one can elevate and amplify one's voice. It's about getting noticed, building and riding momentum and having fun along the way. It's empowerment through expression, which is enhanced further by recognition and respect. It's about letting people know what you represent and what you stand for. There's also a competitive element where battling others sharpens your skills and also wins you respect, acknowledgement and admiration. It's about making a name for yourself through your exceptional skill in your chosen medium (rap, dance, DJ, graffiti etc.). At a community level, this is very empowering, serving mostly to elevate often marginalised, oppressed and under-represented communities. Hip-hop is powerful. It has changed and continues to change the world. It definitely changed my life. It turned a shy, insecure child who hated the spotlight into a confident, grounded man who feels most himself when he's performing on stage in front of thousands of people.

Internally, I sometimes find myself navigating the shades

of grey between these two parts of me like a sea captain trying to make sense of a chart that is full of complex riddles. I strive to be what I never had as a kid: an uncompromising Sikh in the entertainment world who I could have related to. But then there's that nuance again. I've learned that Sikhi doesn't care about representation. It doesn't care whether it's a minority or whether it fits in with the mainstream. Imagine how this duality plays out within me. An endless mediating of thoughts and feelings, internal conflicts that manifest in daily decision-making about whether I accept a gig offer or television appearance, or what I say in a song or interview. Some say that's pressure. I say that's what it's like to be me.

In my efforts to try to appease people's curiosity about how hip-hop and Sikhi have fit within my life to the point where I've chosen to pursue a career as a rapper, I have most definitely done a disservice to both by trying to relate or compare the two. All that people need to know when they see a Sikh man in a hoodie with fly kicks behind a mic on stage is that this is who he is.

2pac's 'Changes' still has relevance for me today. I reference the first two lines of the second verse in my song 'Village Boy', which makes a point about the tragic ongoing epidemic of farmer suicides in Panjab. That song put me on the path of self-discovery and self-mastery through hip-hop music. It inspired an opportunity for me to come to terms with who I am and how to make sense of that given where I live in the world – in Australia, physically disconnected from a precolonial motherland I've only ever known through oral and written storytelling. I no longer fight to reconcile my identity. I am comfortable in who I am. I am trying my best to be a Sikh and at the same time …

> I am hip-hop. It's the essence of me
> It's the genesis, the birth of my Adam and Eve
> No temptation, there is no apple to eat
> Unless you give me a mic to lay a rap on the beat
> Even then, I will tackle the beast, I am rap
> The poetical cat, that'll shatter MCs
> I stay ahead of the pack coz I know who I be
> I'll never be a slave even if they shackle my feet
> I am free, for days I can go on
> There is no mic I can't flow on, it's time to get the show on
> While these rappers chasing bread tryna get their dough on
> I plant my feet in the ground and try to get my grow on
> I am the streets, the dope fiends and addicts
> I am knowledge, from science to mathematics
> I am spiritual and lyrical, beyond political
> I'm one with the people but I'm still individual
> I Am …

NOTHING REMEMBERED AND EVERYTHING THAT WAS

Declan Fry

And each tree shouldering its share of ice, moon steadying, branches of birches waving and shrugging in the train window – brief, like the shadows of the moon, the train's motion continually disappearing them again – and as we sped on I thought of the last message you had left, Aline, the one inviting me to stay at your home, and it occurred to me that you were, or would be, the first person I could truly say I had met, here in Holland, having arrived in Amsterdam two days before – the first person I would come to know.

Your message had appeared in my inbox early last week, in the morning; I remember it because of how the light shone that day, it felt like the whole world was giving in to summer; by seven am most of my desk lay bathed in sunlight, the motes illuminated in a beam arrowing its way across the ceiling; I had just come from the shower, brushing my teeth – waiting for the computer to restart, as if being there might hasten it – while the cursor of the mouse, wavering and flashing, gave way to your message; and I had to return to the bathroom; and even in those few moments I took to glance over your reply I could tell it was affirmative, that you had said yes to my request – *Will you be available to host me in Alkmaar?* – sent a few weeks before; the third line of your reply contained details elaborating further upon the generalities of your couchsurfing profile, a profile which informed prospective travellers, in clear but invitingly nonchalant terms, whereabouts in Holland it was that you lived, detailing the route to your second-storey apartment at length, adding that, in the Netherlands, the street level represents the ground floor, just in case anyone coming from those countries where things are otherwise might benefit from this proviso.

I remember stepping down from the train, my feet adjusting to the slippery glimmer of cement, hand upon the rail of the platform staircase at Alkmaar; I remember the snow leading up to the houses, a snow so pure and white it seemed no presence had ever entered it, constantly renewing itself upon the ground; the effect was to make those ahead of me look as if they had never been, they seemed to glide just above the earth, everything buried almost as soon as it was made; beside me a young girl, crouched, head cradled against the receiver of her phone, communing with someone; ahead of her another young woman – curious, hesitant, faintly sceptical – hurrying forward; I stared up at the sky and back again at the ground and could not tell one from the other. The only way I had of knowing what lay ahead was to walk, having double-checked the folds of the map inside my pocket – the one I had brought from the hostel I was staying at in the Gouden Straatjes, in Haarlem; although it may have been Bos en Lommer, I had boarded the train for Alkmaar there – a map I imagined you, Aline, must have given to other travellers who had visited before me; guests you told me you had hosted, leading them to where you lived; It'll be directly facing you when you leave from the south exit, you had told me; I saw now that there was a row of two-storey apartment buildings – aqua blue, moss green, lights glimmering through the snow, the soft and delicate sheen demarcating one balcony from the next – and a strangely curved street, each end retreating down a long road disappearing into the dark, the outlines of cars parked either side vanishing; as I stepped closer, I saw one brought to life, its headlights slicing through the black before shouldering a curb and angling away, heard the groan and clamour of the engine as the driver accelerated, could almost see them through the fogged window, eased forward in their seat, negotiating a bend before discreetly swivelling and gliding off into the soft snow.

The apartment building was two storeys. You lived on the second floor – I remembered that detail from your initial message – Second Floor, Stationsweg, Alkmaar Station.

On the landing of your address a man, clutching a hat – a kind of felt grey bowler hat, his body enveloped in a plaid coat – found me struggling my luggage up the stairs; he reached out, took the handle from me, raising the bag up while his other hand leveraged itself against the bannister – called upon for support, it creaked in protest – and, having just begun to close the door to his own apartment, he pulled my suitcase up to where he stood, ready, it seemed to me, to leave, to go out somewhere, although where in Alkmaar – when any question of destination in this unknown city was, to me, an open one – I could not say; it was as if we were both lost, in a place where everything commanded an equal share of anonymity; around each object lay a – to me – only vague sense of purpose, one that, despite my having only been there a short time, hid in every aspect of the language, the vehicles, the clothing, and inside of every building into which people hurried and vanished, freed of clear meaning or import – the feeling was so strong I could not help wondering what apartments really were – what were businesses, what were restaurants? – it was obscure, not least this particular building, a green and quiet place whose colour was only slightly darker than the moss of a billiards table, and inside of which I now stood, waiting with bowler hat.

Directing his gaze away from my luggage to me and back, he asked, Are you lost?, and placed a hand inside of his pocket, feeling about for something – a reminder or missing object – until his hand reappeared, a small greyish slip of paper between his fingers. He unwrapped it in his right hand, the fingers working in isolation, and I noticed, as it crinkled and drew apart, a lowering glint, the flash of a wedding band. Pointing from me to his paper – as if I might have lost it – he said, or seemed to ask, Is this the address you're looking for? It took me a moment to realise he was speaking to me in English; everyone I had seen or tried speaking to since arriving had spoken Dutch – and even then only cautiously, as if caught out, wearied by the act or invitation to have to speak with someone visibly foreign – always that undecided scepticism in their voice whenever they began to speak – and yes, it was true that I felt in those hints something being assumed beneath their breath, something they did not mean for me to catch – a raised hand or eyebrow, a furtive sideways look, a sceptical double-take, assimilating and assessing my appearance – so that, when I replied to bowler hat, I said simply, The address, and glanced down, hoping to identify some word both from my memory of your invitation and the crinkles concealing what I took to be your handwriting – blue ink, dimly visible within the folds of the greying paper – while bowler hat stood playing sentry, looking languorous and grimly ironic. He smiled, said, This might be it, and then: Here, pointing, as if that confirmed everything, or at least the reason for our both being there; somehow I felt like I was still trying to buy time – my hand was in my pocket and searching for a phone, anything to confirm where it was I was supposed to be, all the while kicking myself for not having checked everything beforehand, the location, how to find your address, even just a second time before I had gotten off the train – and now bowler hat, still smiling and pointing toward the door beside us, the one directly opposite my luggage, was saying There, there, it's there, and nodding, as if it were a joke or simply that he had been looking for you and, with the aid of my arrival, suddenly realised where you were meant to be.

Knocking at the entrance, having thanked him, finding the door to your home oddly heavy and, as I waited, realising that I could not hear anything from inside, wondering if anyone was there, whether they could hear what was happening outside – because it seemed strange, the more I thought about it, that nothing, not even a floorboard, was audible from where I stood; it was so unlike the hosts I had previously met, people who offered their homes to couchsurfers and would never think of letting someone arrive at their house unannounced – because that was what I had begun to worry, that maybe you had forgotten – and, really, that was not the only thing: there was also the fact that you had not come, despite the protesting staircase, despite bowler hat, from wherever you were inside of your apartment, even *just in case*, even *just checking*, even *knowing* it may or may not have been me, a guest arriving.

Perhaps the complex was used to noise, to unexpected visitors and the hushed murmurs of stairs and neighbours having it out in the adjoining floors and rooms.

Hello?

Your voice was not quite hesitant, not quite unassuming – inquisitive, I think, cautiously inquiring – and the door was suddenly being prised open, your fingers – nails unpainted – curled round it; you were glancing somewhere behind me – I heard bowler hat arrive at the stairwell entry, push open the front door, something I could not see, only hear, the murmur of the door being cracked ajar, wind rushing in – I remembered your name then, Aline – and the accompanying rush of bowler hat making his way out into the snow, a faint slushing like shoes sifting through wet gravel; and I saw the realisation in your eyes, as if everything up until this moment had been a half-remembered film or foreign language and now, now, you had begun to recognise it as your own, something familiar and anticipated.

Oh god, you said, you're here. I nodded, feeling somehow as if I were apologising – I had trouble, I said. That's okay, you said, it was *all fine*; and I had the impression you were about to say something else, too, as I stepped inside – still sensing that I was interrupting, even as you ushered me in – before asking you whether I should take my shoes off; Oh, yes, you said, and raised a finger, as if to indicate having caught some stray thought or reminder, something you'd forgotten to mention – I mean, you don't have to, you added; then: So I guess you can keep them on if you like. I said it was okay, and you nodded, retrieving a pair of indoor slippers from an alcove set into the wall beside the front door, before apologising: Of course, you weren't sure if they were my size.

Placing my feet upon the floorboards I felt something begin to make sense, become familiar or acquainted about my surroundings; you were standing in the half-light; directly facing us was a long, semi-circular window, through which the street outside – I could distinguish the faint bristle of lights along the road – was visible; to the right, a kitchen, something steaming on the stove, the filmy shimmer against the bricks indicating that you had been in the middle of cooking when I arrived; the smell, I think you could say, was vaguely briny – mussels, or scallops; the fleshy scent of prawns – and you told me, later, that you felt, with me being Australian, at least in some sense, and since you knew a little of that country – your brother was studying there – that it might remind me of home. Above it all, there was a low, whirring roar, which, I began to understand, was the hum of cars outside, muffled now by layers of snow – Months of it, you said after I asked; It's been falling for ages now – and which appeared, through the semi-circular window, as a tissue of white, moving through the mauve indigo illuminating both the window and the frame – a kind of architrave – beside two of the other windows I could see, one of which, I realised, formed a sort of balcony outside your bedroom, while the other, just opposite – a pane of semicircular glass inlaid toward the ceiling, maybe three quarters of the way up the wall – housed a small vase containing a yellow flower – I remember it looked like a Dutch iris – lilting toward the light from the kitchen.

How was your trip? you asked. I told you about the train ride, recalling the shuffle of the carriage through snow, the buildings hovering in and out of visibility; it was maybe the first montage I learnt to recognise here, something I associated with childhood, when my father would drive my brother and me thirty or forty kilometres through Xi'an into town; as I grew older I learnt to take comfort in this, the stream of landscape rolling past a window; and aboard the trams I discovered, moving to Melbourne – where a film of buildings, trees, streets, people dimly rushed past each day during the morning commute – that it was true, movement made everything familiar; or rather in movement the world, if you cared enough to notice, became closer – an accommodating intimacy, I think I told you – in your glance there was a surprise, a registering when I used that word, *intimacy*; I said that it was *intimate* or even *intimately familiar* but later understood that it was *accommodation* I had been thinking of, an *accommodating intimacy*, as I described those trips with my father and brother and you nodded, in what I took to be your own kind of accommodation; so I continued telling you how, despite this feeling, this experience that I was describing to you – the shuffling of the train, Dutch language echoing through the carriages, sparse landscape, an endless reel – everything was still impenetrable and distant just outside of the window, and each house situated so far apart from the next that the train felt less like it was moving than that it was circling some fixed point in the snow, zeroing in on home after home it could never quite reach; hearing this, you nodded, smiled – I had the sense I was boring you, or, if not, that you were humouring me or just being polite; probably I was rambling; yet despite this I felt there was still some curiosity, some degree of attention or desire to know – to know what, I wasn't exactly sure – so I kept talking about these trips, me and my brother in the back seat, and not wearing seatbelts because, our father had told us, you really didn't need to, not unless you were in the front or in the middle of the car – the seat in front, he'd say, was protection enough in the event of a crash – and you laughed, asked, So how was it, getting here? Did you have trouble finding the place? I told you about bowler hat, about the piece of paper with your address scrawled across it – Crinkled, it was really pretty crinkled, I said, but left out the part I had imagined, which was that the paper was so far gone that I saw it crack and fall to pieces, and you said, Yes, he's been using that one for a while; you had made it for him. I asked if you had many guests come and you explained that there were a few every month or so, but that you needed a break; your neighbour next door – bowler hat – He doesn't actually wear it all the time, you said, Only sometimes, when he goes out – he had gotten used, you said, to giving travellers directions to your apartment; took pleasure in it, even, catching them as they trudged through the snow, coming up from the station; on those occasions, you said, he would show people the way to your apartment, guiding them up the stairs – He's semi-retired, you said, Really he's just happy to meet so many new people, hear new languages and see different relationships; you said you had hosted friends travelling together over the summer holidays, university students, couples of every conceivable description – And his wife, you said, she's an avid traveller, or was – she passed three years ago, around this time – Perhaps, you said, there was more to it than simple curiosity or pleasure, novelty, in meeting all of these people. I asked if you hosted many couchsurfers travelling alone; It was the first thing I noticed, I said, when you confirmed that you would host me; true, I had met women, women living with other people, women who had offered to put me up for a night after having a met a couple of times socially, over lunch or with friends; but this was different, this was the first time that a woman, someone I had never met – someone living alone – had offered to let me stay. Whether because you had not heard my question or because you were ignoring it, you briefly disappeared into the kitchen before reemerging, carrying a pot over to the dining table; I thought you might be taking a moment to answer, since you began, gently, to laugh; but when you spoke it was only to ask again if I had had trouble finding the place, Many have trouble, you said, and then: I forgot to ask – oh, I'm really sorry – I didn't ask if you were allergic to anything. I said it was fine, there was nothing I couldn't eat; Well, I hope you like marinara soup, you said – and I noticed you didn't say chowder, whether because you didn't use that expression or because they didn't call it chowder here – then: Have you couchsurfed much? Rallying off some names, I said, A few places, recalling relationships that had developed, over weeks or days, messages back and forth, plus the cities I'd visited, or still wanted to; and always, as I spoke, trying to gauge your reaction, because nothing I said seemed to intrude on you; everything was met with a kind of uniform tolerance; yet somehow this was less odd than the simple happiness of that uniformity – horizonless, strange, subdued, as if anything

I said would have made you happy, if happiness was what it was. Had she travelled anywhere herself? Oh no, no! I prefer hosting, you said. It feels safer. Yes, I said, And it depends on where you go, doesn't it? You admitted to me then that many of the places you would prefer to visit weren't the easiest to travel in: Lagos. Nicaragua. Bolivia. Cuba. My brother, you said, even used to say that I should visit North Korea. Staring down at your meal, you added: But I never did. And something about this thought seemed to stop you; you paused, your gaze directed to somewhere just beyond my plate; you finished your meal and, as you raised your head, I sensed that you were looking past me. I could not see anything outside, but to say something, anything at all, in that silence, would have seemed rude; so I found myself silently joining you, as you stared out through the glass into the snow of Alkmaar, where nothing separated the earth and the sky and in all the world the only moving thing was the snow continuously falling. If I focused, I found I could detect a kind of divide in the window, a divide marked by the Dutch iris. You must be looking forward to seeing him, I said. Turning to face me you said, simply:

Actually, he died.

In that moment I felt, hearing those words, all of the things I would later have to forget or dismiss – preconceptions, assumptions, dozens of thoughts – slowly rise and fall away, followed in turn by the dismissal of things I did not even realise I had been thinking; I offered to help you clear away the plates, because in that moment I really had nothing else, I suppose, to offer – you waved a hand, brushed off the idea; and I knew that this was not the first obligatory dismissal you had been asked to summon in conversation with a stranger – and maybe friends, too – but another polite disclaimer, a shrugging-off, all part of the requirement, the demand of having to accommodate others as they arrived at a place that was never meant for them.

That night, before we went to bed, at your suggestion, we watched a film, *L'eclisse*; I remember nothing except my surprise that everything should be suspended, watching this film together, and watching too for any sign of incomprehension or subdued expectation, of feeling like I should be doing something, as if there was an obscure need I could answer, something you wanted but would not say, sitting with your feet up, staring at the pale blue of the TV screen; it was something I could almost touch, and all the more so because I could not see it, had no idea what we were doing in front of the TV after what you had just told me – but also no idea if the conversation that we were not having was what it really was, or if it was just me needing to take on some role I probably couldn't – or wouldn't – sustain, as if everyone might have it in them to suddenly turn friend or confidante if required; all I knew was that I had the ability, or the chance – or the permission – to be there beside you, briefly, with thoughts I owed to you to keep to myself, ideas which I felt made no sense to voice, and which I had not even begun to understand – especially since I was not the one, as you were, who had asked for understanding.

Actually, he died. In Australia.

The film ended; we went to our separate rooms. Lying in bed I could see – through the entrance, just down the passage connecting us – that you had left the door to your room open; whether purposely or not, I had no way of knowing, but wondered if it was just a habit, one you had no intention of interrupting for my sake. Yet forgetfulness or nonchalance couldn't explain the discomfort I felt, perceiving this sense of invitation – a clear passage and an opening, the hallway leading to your room easily accessible from where I lay; what made it stranger was that I could *hear* you – or someone in the adjoining apartment – crying. I placed my ear to the wall and noticed how the sound rose, convincing me that it must have come from your room; except that, since the sound dimmed before returning, it became harder to tell if it really was your room or the next; between the two of us lay the passage, a door and, through that door, a world as visible as if my eyes were closed and imagining it – as I could see you, lying there – and trying, with my ear pressed against the wall, to envisage each of these two different scenarios: one in which you were crying, one in which the sound came from the neighbouring apartment; wanting to feel which was the more believable, when every part of me was certain it could only have been you. But maybe I had only convinced myself of this, knowing that you lay somewhere on the other side of that darkness, and looking somewhere I could only guess at, perhaps hearing the same sounds as me or, if they did belong to you, wondering whether I could hear them too. Focused on this thought, asking myself if you would be disappointed in my lack of response – if you expected me to come to your room; if you expected me, in some way, to be with you – I drifted, sinking down into a darkness so clear it felt as though I was stepping inside of it.

The next morning you suggested we take a trip to the coast; inside the car I looked toward you and imagined, through the snow and slate-grey sky – a sky that gave nothing back, no reflection, only the pale illumination of your fingertips guiding the steering wheel as we drove – that your face might still be the same one I had imagined last night; and I found it strange, thinking this – that *I had to imagine* – when I did not have to imagine anything, because *it was all there*; but that was what it felt like, that I had to imagine you, had to imagine your eyes trained up toward the ceiling and staring, the only things reflecting the light from the hallway – just as now the only glinting appearances in the landscape were the houses, pastel blue and postbox red; and a faint yellow, too, like the flower you kept behind glass inside the alcove of your window; recalling how later you had told me it was not a Dutch iris at all but a native Australian iris; *Patersonia xanthina*, you'd said, pronouncing the name like any ordinary thing; and I'd wondered, but had not asked, how it ended up in your house – imagining all this was part of the same face that had stared up toward the ceiling while a trickle of light fell across the mattress and I fought the urge to leave my bed and walk into your room and say *Aline*; only of course there was no tear, or at least no way of knowing, only my urging it into existence based on what I thought I had heard that night, somewhere through the wall – but it could have been next door, above or below; it could have been your room; it could have been you – I was startled, and yet not enough, I think, for you to notice. You asked me – as if you had stepped out of the present and into my head – how I had slept last night; Great, I said, but also: They really help in this weather, the thicker rugs. It's nice, isn't it, you said, having ones like that. Cosy. And then you said, I guess you must be looking forward to seeing your parents in … Australia? China? I couldn't remember if I had told you I lived with my parents, but when I mentioned this – although it had not been my intention – you said, Sorry, and then, I'm not sure what I was thinking, I don't know why I assumed. After a pause, you said: I thought maybe you had told me you lived with them. It's my mistake. I lived with mine – and Pieter, my brother – before I moved back. Guess I'm just projecting. I said, Peter? Because it was true that you hadn't mentioned him directly last night – only referred to him as your brother – and it was equally true, I realised, that your parents, too, were just *My parents*. Nameless, as if they could have belonged to anyone. I found myself looking out the window as the car began to turn, and again I saw the pale outline reflected on your side, your fingers transparent, guiding us off into this new street – a sign reading *Naaktstrand Bergen* – the houses reminding me through the otherwise indistinguishable whiteness of snow that we were travelling; and I realised I had never sat inside of a car that handled like yours, inaudibly drifting, while the buildings receded and gave way to an ashen landscape of cafés and streetlights; and through the backdrop of receding towns a receding world, all outlines and vanishing curves – homes half-disappeared; a road truncated – I say *backdrop* but perhaps what I really saw, or felt, was only whiteness, the unidentifiable colour of it, of snow and the enveloped city, snow that fell and kept on falling – but bottoming out, too – and a world flourishing against what we could, or might still, be capable of seeing; because we were being ushered back, into the past, along with all of its fears and complaints and adjudications about what could still be accomplished and what never would, the way a trip strikes out for somewhere implausible and yet-to-be and may still land somewhere beyond that, somewhere we never meant to end up, deeper than any previous plan could have carried us; at first I thought we were turning onto another highway, but as your car rose and the ground began to level I saw, through the passenger window, what had been running beside us this whole time, the streets of what you told me was a place whose exact name I no longer remember; I could smell brine, the sea, the tang of shells and umbrellas and plastic, but was unsure how much of it belonged to *Naaktstrand Bergen* and how much to a memory superimposed from elsewhere, layered atop that cold landscape, where the ocean eased back from the rocks along the pier as we drove; outside of my window the shore riding back, waves collapsing and retiring, something no longer able to accommodate them and so they begin again, wave after wave, slow, solemn lacing and retracing as I paused, easing, and found myself watching you; so that what came to me, eventually, was not a memory of the beaches in Melbourne but the fact of us being there, after all these weeks of travel; sitting beside you, Aline, detecting something in the smell of the sea that was vegetal and faintly grassy – the scent of rocks, perhaps, somewhere rising angular and jagged and darkly visible through the snow that was only now returning – I could see the pier, and I could see, too, the pools of water in the rocks either side, but could not tell what it was – the smell of food, of seafood – wondering now if maybe you had packed some beforehand, leftovers from last night; until you turned to me, as if expecting me to ask you this exact question – that I was wondering where we were, and what it was you wanted to say – while the car, slowing, pulled in toward the pier, and a van emerged, a van so small and fragile it seemed almost to tilt in the wind, its crenellated beach umbrella awnings bookended by menu prices etched in chalk – a roadside seafood vendor – and I could see two silver pots sweating between the awnings – the smell of marinara soup, white but with a kind of clear transparency – and I turned to ask you, Aline, something that, even as I was saying it, felt uncertain, shameful, but in that moment the urge to ask you overwhelmed any sense of discomfort or embarrassment, so that it wasn't really a surprise when you turned to me, almost as if you were expecting to be asked, and, as uncertain as I was to be posing the question – Did your brother make it? – I saw something unknown travel across your face, vanishing almost as soon as it appeared – so that maybe there was no flash, no flash and therefore no vanishing – while you looked toward me and I knew that whether you had said *yes* or you had said *no*, the answer had already been there, that *something else* – that there was no *yes* and there was no *no*, there was only *something else* – until I changed the question and asked, Did he like it?, as if that clarified things; but it clarified nothing, least of all the fact that what I really wanted to ask you was, Did you cook for him?, but you remained silent and, turning, I understood – as presumptuous as it seems to say now, of course, but somehow, somehow, I knew – that if there ever was an answer I had lost the chance to hear it.

You were steering the car back, in the direction we had just come, the vendor's truck appearing now on your side as you stepped out and I, following, watched you order two serves of marinara; I asked that mine not be spicy and you told me that neither were; you asked me if I would like to walk down to the shore with you – maybe to visit one of the piers – because you had parked the car just off to the side of the road and it was true that, as you said to me then, the marinara might cool faster if we walked and ate, and I said, Sounds like a plan, the steam from the soup rising and reminding me how far away last night seemed, almost as if it had happened to some other person, someone I had once known and even now had trouble remembering; this other person had sat with you, Aline, whom I had been with for barely a day and would probably never see again; we had both known him in some way, one of us perhaps with more confidence than the other – I imagine that sounds arrogant to you, but that was what I thought, even if it was a strange thought, really – and this smell of marinara soup seemed, even then, like a common bond between us, a shared recollection, and I said to you, It's funny, memories sometimes seem like memories before they've really become them, glancing up as you tested your soup, steam rising from the blue-white paper bowl; Maybe you experience memory as something far away, you said; in my mind I heard myself thinking, *near but distant*, Like walking into a room and forgetting why you went there, you added, But who knows? What do you think?; I laughed and said, Nothing. Actually, I said, looking up at you, I was really only thinking out loud. You smiled, Who doesn't do that? you said, raising the broth to your lips and blowing it a little, sending ripples across the surface. I said, You know, it's been a while since I had the space to think like this – feeling like I was about to thank you or perhaps tell you I was grateful – in my head I imagined the words, *Thank you, Aline* – and with them imagined also this way of saying your name for the first time, really saying it, and hoping both that you would and wouldn't ask me what I was thinking, this idea of telling you, this honesty of saying *I was just thinking of your name* or that I was only thinking of saying it because of realising that I never had – but all of it seemed too much after last night; and I still couldn't recognise, in your face, or in anything you said, what had really happened then; so I didn't say anything to you, but instead kept walking, my breath urging the soup toward the lip of the cup, sharing something I was still not sure of the associations of, or if there were any at all; perhaps the suggestions were all mine, an endless hypothesising and surmising about what may or may not have been real, worrying any certainty away until suddenly you asked me: How old is your brother?, and I said, Five years younger than me, he's eighteen; It's funny that you start with your age difference, you said, and I realised that you were right, it was funny – or maybe it was only your suggestion that made it seem that way. I was grateful when you laughed, happy to be sharing this small unclear comedy between us, another joke or impulse I could not tell if we were exchanging or simply bound to, whether as a matter of politeness or reciprocal embarrassment; but in that moment I could believe that we were in a way tougher and more devoted, making something up between us, talking about our siblings, than we had been last night, committed to sharing an idea, something up until then unspoken; and as you finished your soup and threw away the container I noticed that you really were crying while the day turned cold and the snow picked up and you were crying into the napkin I held out to you as you turned away from me, you wiped your eyes, you cradled your mouth and, inside of your coat, the endless snow, you fell; my free hand found and caught you and my soup was on the ground then, too, steam rising from the snow while you searched for my shoulder as the seagulls turned and flashed grey above us, dipping toward the horizon, somehow the horizon I imagined as you told me, you told me, that you were sorry, only there was no horizon, there was only you saying you were sorry, only sky and it was not the weather we should have been walking in that day, you said, not the weather when there was no horizon, no horizon and therefore no sky, only sun filled with weather, with squawking and a shore rushing on as the gulls rise until there is no line between them and no line between us, nothing dividing horizon and nothing dividing sea, only the edge of a world slowly vanishing, there, toward the sunrise, toward a place where everything, in its urge to begin, ends.

GR8FUL

Shankari Chandran

In the final stages of the radio show host's tirade, Anji pulled into the nursing-home car park. She'd never listened to 2WMR before and hadn't even known how to tune her car radio to find it. Her twin, Siddharth, had messaged her from London to tell her to ignore it.

The WMR in 2WMR stands for White Men Rule, he'd joked during their recent and increasingly frequent messages. They had a WhatsApp group with Amma and their partners, but this exchange was a private thread, so Anji could tell Sid the truth without upsetting their mother.

It was hard to hide the truth from Amma, though. The news – if Anji could call it that – was on every TV channel, on social media, the radio, and now on the outer walls of their nursing home.

Gareth had thrown away their friendship and brought a formal complaint against the nursing home for racism. His grounds for the complaint were that her family had removed an old statue of Captain Cook from the home's front garden. In addition to this 'hate crime' Anji had had the audacity to employ too many non-White people and take on too many non-White elderly residents.

The conciliation at the tribunal was supposed to be confidential but extracts of Gareth's complaint had started to be quoted on the radio. Clearly someone had leaked it. Anji turned off the car and turned the volume on Mick 'Jonno' Johnson down a notch. As the owner of a diverse portfolio of assets – including part of an AFL team in Victoria, a health spa in Byron Bay and a sheep station in South Australia – Jonno appealed to a broad cross-section of the bigoted. She was sure he hammed up his ocker accent; the twang was too inconsistent, the use of idioms too frequent. No one who'd been educated at Shore Grammar School, holidayed in Courchevel and lived in Woollahra said, 'Struth, mate.' No one born after 1950 or who was not a character in a quirky Australian comedy said, 'Struth, mate.' She doubted anyone had ever really said, 'Struth, mate!' except in the imagination of the true-blue mind.

The shock jock's rhetoric was building towards its climax. 'Don't get me wrong, I love Indians. I love their curries and they're damn fine cricketers. Really good at IT too. If I need someone to fix my wi-fi, I'll call an Indian.' Anji exhaled deeply. 'But twenty years ago, there were less than a hundred thousand Indian people here. Now, there are almost five hundred thousand Indians. That's *half a million*! They're here, taking our education.'

Subsidising our education actually, Anji thought.

'Taking our jobs.'

Were they really?

'Everyone knows they only employ their own.'

Ah, that old chestnut.

Jobs for the boys – who'd have thought that could be so offensive in this country, where most CEOs were the fourth generation educated in the same sandstone neo-Oxbridge colleges and quadrangles as their colleagues?

'And that's what's pushed this poor guy over the edge. He's just saying what we're all thinking; what we're all feeling inside but are too afraid of the political correctness police to say aloud.'

Where were these political correctness police throughout her time at school and university, her early years at hospital? Why weren't they issuing fines to consultants who congratulated her for being so brave and progressive because she got an education, married a White boy and didn't wear a hijab? And the doctors who kept asking her, 'Where are you from?' and responded to her answer ('I'm from Westgrove') with, 'No, where are you *really* from?'

Once, a junior doctor had asked her if her children played cricket. When she answered no, that Kailash, Hari and Rishi preferred soccer like their father, he'd said, 'But it must be in their blood?' She'd replied, trying to smile: 'Not so much. Do *your* children have genocidal or criminal tendencies in their blood?' In her upward-appraisal, the doctor had provided feedback that she was 'overly sensitive and lacked interpersonal skills and humour'.

The host of 2WhiteMenRule took a deep breath, refilling his lungs with air, getting ready to convert that air into hatred and fear. 'I love this country, and I welcome people to it, people who share our values. For those who come across the seas, we've boundless plains to share.' *Surely, he had not just quoted the national anthem.* 'But these foreigners, who are escaping their shithole countries, come here and, like I said yesterday, they are a parasite, a cancer on Australia. We're trying to hold back the tide here, mate, with nothing but a boogie board to keep the rest of us afloat.' *A boogie board?* She imagined Jonno sitting astride a boogie board in his budgie smugglers wearing an Akubra and sunscreen-based war paint across his face. They, them and the rest of us. Immigrants were no more tribal than the locals.

'This nursing home has gone too far,' he said. There it was. The reminder about Cinnamon Gardens. Her heart pounded painfully in her chest, a wild animal clambering to escape the threat. Danger was closing in and her limbic system was in a constant state of fight-or-flight. She tried to visualise her reptile brain and envelop it in a pink, soothing light, the way her husband taught schoolchildren during his counselling sessions.

'Fuck that,' she said out loud. Pink light wasn't going to help her.

'This nursing home, which has benefitted from federal grants, which is supposed to look after some of the most vulnerable people in our community' – *God, he was making it sound like they were torturing old people* – 'has taken that money and that trust and, instead of being grateful, they spit on this country. This country which has given its owners refuge and a commercially successful business.' Australia didn't *give* them more than it gave any other small business owner. And they had given back over the four decades since her parents had moved here and become taxpayers. 'I repeat, when you tear down a founding father of this country, you spit on its foundation. If you spit on this country, you spit on everything the Anzacs fought for.' *The Anzacs?* Anji shook her head. When had they come into this? She bloody loved the Anzacs. They received a veteran's discount at Cinnamon Gardens. Jonno continued. 'You spit on all of us. And we will spit back.'

After yesterday's *Jonno in the Morning*, and its 3pm repeat, #foreignparasites and #foreigncancer had begun trending. At sunrise, Ruben, the nursing home caretaker, had started scrubbing the words *parasite* and *cancer* off the outside walls. Anji's personal favourite was *Cook killer*. Tomorrow they could look forward to some variation of *spit* on the walls, no doubt. She had to admire Jonno's approach. Short, simple catchphrases, repeated on a loop.

She walked from the car park down the driveway to the outer wall. Ruben was still working. Soap foam flecked his dark skin and curly black hair. The pressure hose had taken off several layers of the graffiti but she could see the imprint, like a faded tattoo.

'I asked you to stop. In fact, I didn't ask you to start this job,' she said to him. He often didn't listen to her requests to stop working so hard and quietly just took care of all the odd jobs around the nursing home that needed attention 'There's worse to come. I think we should just leave it up. Shame these idiots by leaving it there for everyone to see,' she said, turning off the hose at the tap.

'These idiots have no shame,' he replied, standing back to assess his progress. 'I didn't want your mother to see it.'

She nodded, her throat tight and painful.

'*Jonno in the Morning* isn't the worst of them, but he's got the loudest microphone, I suppose.' Ruben dried his hands on a small towel and then wiped the sweat from his body under his t-shirt.

'You've been following him?' Anji asked.

'Following is an overstatement. 2WMR is repulsive, but I feel like I need to know what the people are feeling, if only to know what they'll be spray-painting next. Is it bad that I long for the days of *Fuck off bitch*?'

Anji laughed and felt some of the strain in her shoulders and neck ease. 'You didn't like Gareth applauding you at the Commission for availing yourself of Australia's fine education system?' she teased.

He grimaced. 'There was a lot about Gareth at the Commission I didn't like. To be honest, there's a lot about Gareth anywhere that I don't like. That said, he has reason to dislike me too.'

'Yes, I hear you. But that particular comment?'

He shrugged. 'I was educated largely in Sri Lanka. Jaffna University, before the war, was an excellent institution. My education wasn't driven by Western opportunities. All Tamils study hard. They want an education and, in the past, it's been the only thing that saved us.'

He soaked a steel-wool scrubber in the bucket of water. 'Although, I'm washing walls and he's probably recruiting an agent to help publish his future memoir.'

'If he calls it, *You've Taken Everything*, I'm going to scream,' Anji said.

Ruben laughed and returned to work.

The next day, the nursing home's outer wall was covered in the words *we spit on you* and *ungr8ful bitch*. The word *bitch* always scared her. It seemed more personal than all the others she'd read on her wall. As though the author of that word could see her through the brick barrier that surrounded the nursing home. As though he was watching her and hating her even more than the allegedly racist nursing home itself.

She stood on the footpath, looking at the fuzzy spray-painted lines and letters in erratic sizes and angles but consistent in their accusation. Ruben had finally agreed to leave the graffiti there, at least until she emailed today's photos to the police, so they could ignore them like they had yesterday's photos and the photos from the day before that.

Ungrateful. She *was* grateful to Australia for the refuge it had offered her family. She had never been ungrateful for that. She. Was. Gr8ful. But she had started to hate that word over the years. *You should be grateful, Anji; grateful that you've been able to build a life here in Australia. Grateful for all the opportunities this country has given you. Grateful that you've been able to do so well.* So grateful to Australia that you were not allowed to criticise it. She'd heard that so many times from so many people: well-meaning, casually racist people who would never themselves feel such vertiginous levels of gratitude for the same opportunities, because they were somehow entitled to them, while she wasn't. Opportunity and refuge: the privilege of the migrant Australian. Our lifelong responsibility and debt to be repaid. Opportunity and refuge: the entitlement of the White Australian. Your lifelong expectation.

Absorbed in tracking the words across the wall, she didn't notice the woman pushing a pram towards her until the woman drew close. Anji turned and smiled. The baby was leaning forward, one hand on the safety bar, the other pointing at the sky. There was a little dog tied to the pram, one of those caramel-coloured curly ones that looked like a toy bear. The baby clapped and Anji clapped back.

She glanced at the mother in time to see the woman moving her closed mouth in an elliptical manner, as though something was stuck and spinning inside it. As she passed Anji, the woman opened her mouth and coughed. Anji felt a cold, wet mass hit her cheek and spray across her face. She screamed and raised her hands, too shocked to do or say anything. The woman ran, pushing her pram, its cross-country wheels rattling in front and the little dog stumbling behind her. She picked up the animal, threw it into the pram and sprinted away down the street. Anji wiped the saliva and tears from her face on her sleeve and ran inside to the safety and refuge of her nursing home.

The police officers that attended the scene of the crime arrived in a pair, one male and one female. They were both young and unsure of how to help her. The Westgrove Police Station had not sent its finest, and it had only sent these two because she had called the station repeatedly. She showed them the vandalised wall and the broken CCTV cameras.

'It's not really a crime scene,' Officer Arkell said, flipping his notebook to a blank page. He stood awkwardly in front of the wall, unsure of what to do with his lanky frame.

'It is actually,' Uncle Gana answered. The old Sri Lankan barrister from Room 5 had insisted on attending the police interview as her lawyer, even though he was not actually her lawyer. Uncle Gana had eschewed his plaid sarong and fake Lacoste polo shirt, and dressed up for law enforcement in a starched business shirt, grey slacks and Bata slippers. His hair was immaculately Brylcreemed as always and shone in the mid-morning sun. He stood behind the officer watching him take notes.

'The graffiti on the nursing home wall is malicious damage,' he explained. 'The spitting is a public order offence. Malicious damage attracts a custodial sentence if the damage is severe. Spitting attracts a fine.'

'You're a criminal lawyer?' Officer Newton asked the old man, while she took photos of the words shouting at Anji across her wall. She took her police cap off and placed it on the ground, tendrils of blonde hair escaping her neat braid and curling in the summer humidity.

'Mostly civil law, but I dabble in criminal when the need arises,' Uncle Gana said smartly. He nodded at Anji, prompting her.

She cleared her throat nervously and said, 'This is the third time the graffiti has happened this week, the first time for the spitting, and it won't be the last for either of them. I'd like you to open an investigation.'

'An investigation?' Officer Newton stopped taking photos and looked at her. 'Dr Ali, we log your complaints, but unless we catch someone at it, or have suspects or you identify the kids who are doing this —'

'*Perpetrators* is the word,' Uncle Gana corrected her.

'Right – perpetrators,' Officer Newton said. 'Unless we know who's doing this, there's nothing we can do about it.'

'That's the purpose of an investigation,' Uncle Gana replied.

'I'm sorry, sir, are you Dr Ali's lawyer?' Officer Arkell looked from him to Anji with irritation.

'He is my lawyer, thank you, Officer,' Anji replied. 'And he's right: it's not my job to hand you the perpetrators. It's your job to investigate what's happening here and find them. Walk the streets, knock on doors and ask questions. Tell people, tell the whole neighbourhood, that you're watching them. Tell them that vandalism and spitting aren't acceptable, that they're crimes.'

Do your fucking job, she thought.

Officer Arkell shut his notebook and took a deep breath. 'Look, Dr Ali, I know it's hard. This seems like a really nice place and you seem like a really nice lady – I mean doctor. It's just that, I don't think you want us stirring up the neighbourhood.'

'I'm not asking you to stir them up; I'm asking you to investigate them, or look at the CCTV footage at the train station and see who's coming into Westgrove at night. If we're lucky, they'll be openly and brazenly carrying cans of spray paint because they know they can vandalise with impunity, if they hit the right homes.'

'Look, it's not like that.'

'I think it's exactly like that, Officer,' she replied, her voice trembling. She hated that tremble. It made her sound weak.

'Don't apologise,' Uncle Gana had coached her. 'Do not plead when asking for your rights as a citizen. If they refuse, then you can take it up the line if you want, but don't give them a way out. Don't be deferential and quiet. Don't accept it.' She could see him looking at her now, waiting.

She exhaled. 'I think if this were the local fish-and-chip shop, run by Mr and Mrs Desmond who make killer calamari rings, you'd be canvassing the neighbourhood like you were Gary Sweet in *Blue Heelers*. I think you'd care enough to do your job. Even if you didn't care about the Desmonds, you'd do your job. But this is different, I'm different, so your approach is different.'

Officer Arkell opened his mouth and was about to speak but Officer Newton touched his arm lightly and shook her head.

'You are different, Dr Ali. But my colleague Rob is right and he means you no disrespect. What he's trying to say is, if we start knocking on doors, we'll draw more attention to you. We'll make you more of a target instead of less of one. We'll take a look at the station CCTV and see if there's anything suspicious happening at night. But if we ask too many questions, too loudly, we'll stir up trouble. You'll become the problem.'

'I'm pointing out the problem. You're asking me to just shut up?'

'I'm asking you to be patient.'

'Why do we always have to be patient?' Anji asked, her voice splitting and betraying her again. She swallowed hard, trying to imagine her throat relaxing and opening up, releasing the words into the world whole and strong.

The woman shook her head. Her kindness and confusion hurt more than if she'd been a racist dick about it.

'You're telling me *don't cause trouble*?' Anji said. *By defending my rights. Don't cause trouble by asking for what's mine*, she thought. *Don't cause trouble by telling the truth.*

A MOUNTAIN WITHOUT A PEAK

Mohammed Massoud Morsi

I had already died before I came to Australia. I had my face on one of those poorly photoshopped posters plastered to the walls of squalid mould-ridden buildings with the familiar obituary: 'The fighter so-and-so, born in such-and-such, was martyred in heroic battle against the evil forces of Pak Harto (the nickname for Indonesia's former president Suharto).' It was the end of a journey and my death was the only way I could leave. But it was also how I had to end a love story that had begun two years earlier. It was an act of fate. That same fate which, in Darwin years later, told me not to get on a plane back to Aceh. There was nothing left for me to return to in Indonesia. Nur, whose name means light, had beautifully drawn lips and a smile that drew an aura around her face. Nur, with her charcoal eyes and coconut-honey scent, had once been the love of my life. But Nur had already passed. She, her family and the entire village of Lho-Nga were swept out to sea by the tsunami that hit the northern tip of Sumatra in 2004.

That day, as I was about to get on a plane in Darwin, fate demanded I stay. It questioned my fears and my meeting Tanami, who had appeared as an enigmatic, emotional distraction from my quest. Tanami was beautiful, with sky-blue eyes and a seemingly free spirit drawing me towards her in the pull of attraction – a pull with the tenacity to change the course of my journey excavating the past. I remember calling my father from Darwin Airport, telling him I was driving back to Broome to be with her.

'If love is your rudder, truth will follow,' he said. 'Look after yourself, my son, and remember that you will often find the truth in places where you might not be prepared to go.' I could hear my father smiling. I had been away for a long time but as his voice reached me from across the world, he might as well have been standing before me.

Many years prior to my father's omen, before those defining moments of my past, I had fallen in love with an old globe in the corner of our living room on Faisal Street in Suez, Egypt. The brown ball was a present from my uncle Ali who had traded it for his best galabeya during the revolution of '52. I remember making up stories as a child, telling my friends that I'd already been to that strangely shaped piece of land at the bottom of the globe, drawn with the name *New Holland* across. Perhaps fate had Australia marked for me, beyond its borders, across the oceans and in another world.

The first time I met Tanami, her bright blue eyes shone. She had strong and powerful feminine hands. Her posture was like a lioness and her hair a mane of long brown silk. It pulled as the tide does with the sea. But what really drew me in was her smile. Her radiant, starlit smile. The first night we spent together we slipped into a still ocean, emerging back out beneath shooting stars. It was as if time had suddenly slowed down. That night we were so close our breaths mirrored, with our heartbeats vibrating and intertwining. I felt the presence of another soul and perhaps also another world. This time, fate spoke in the language of the immeasurable heaven. I heard a voice as if fate could talk: 'The best thing about climbing a mountain is the climb, not the peak.'

Perhaps fate *could* talk, to tell us why it was bringing two people together. It was my first climb up that mountain. I didn't understand fate at the time, but I do now. I felt the waves of time bouncing in and out across my chest. I remembered my childhood bedroom with the hard cotton-filled bed, where I'd be bathed in my own sweat on blistering-hot Suez summer nights. I recalled that next to my bed there was a small chest of drawers. The top of it was covered with a piece of glass, its edge sharp as a knife. I could have covered the edge with tape but for some unknown reason I left it as it was. Each time I cut myself on it by accident I would wait until a large drop of blood had formed and then taste it. I was told it was the best way to stop bleeding, to savour the crass that keeps us alive.

But that was then. Later, I learned that when climbing a broken mountain, the best way to stop the bleeding is by leaving it to bleed. The poor taste of what courses through my veins is a reminder of everything I cannot see, touch or hear.

The night Tanami and I kissed, I was struck by a sense of longing, a churning sensation, as if my gut had enveloped my heart. It came seemingly out of nowhere. Across the seas, beyond the shores of Australia, I had fallen in love with life but also into the waking of souls and bodies. I had cut myself just as I had begun to climb.

It is strange how fate works. A couple of years before I met Nur and a decade before Tanami, I'd met Greg in Copenhagen, Denmark. This Australian–Ukranian man, dating a blonde Danish sweetheart, worked at a communal after-hours gym on the third floor of a rundown government building. The first time he saw me he smiled.

'Where are you from?' I asked him. 'Danes don't smile.'

When I left Denmark for the umpteenth time, this time with a mint to return to Aceh, I came to Australia to visit Greg first. I had had enough of being asked to open my bag at the shopping centres, show my receipts for items bought from other stores, and of being stopped by cops with hatred lining their faces. There were no bombs in Australia, only looks that killed. It was Greg from Denmark who gave me the number of another Greg in Broome, who offered me a bed for the night as I was making my way to the airport in Darwin. I could have flown but, once again, fate told me to drive. Who knows what would have happened, where I'd be now, had I decided not to listen.

As it happened, the very first time I met Tanami, she opened the door. She was babysitting at Greg's. I felt a rush of adrenalin, a sensation of excitement, and caution. The children were already in bed and it didn't take long before Tanami and I were engaged in lengthy conversation. She told me that she had Aboriginal friends, that Australia wasn't as bad as I had experienced. But I never met any of those friends and I wondered whether it was just her or the entire country which seemed to suffer the absence of empathy. That night, I remembered watching her lips as she spoke. She stretched them in a smile and asked, 'Are you religious?'

I should have said I cherished loneliness that shades life, freedom so infinitely more precious than this world. I should have said I loved all those moments where I'm alone with my God. 'No.'

I would have more time with Allah than I'd ever dreamed of. Perhaps fate had sent me to Australia for that very reason. I was a lonely passenger with an unknown direction, and love is like faith. You just have to surrender and trust it will take you where it takes you. There were plenty of warnings but I was already too far up that mountain to turn around. I was attracted to Tanami, as she pushed and pulled my yin and yang of emotions, pleasure as well as pain coursing through my body. My mind ecstatic with recognition. But there was also something else going on.

For years, I'd lived and worked far off the beaten tracks. Squalid places where life is unfair and often unkempt. I suddenly had the chance, the privilege, to go where the grass was greener. I remembered the globe from childhood and in my mind, I pieced together all the right reasons. That night I went for a walk down to the Indian Ocean. Nur had once told me that the sea was the home of lost angels. I knew I could always find her there.

As a full moon shone, I recalled Nur, her beautifully drawn lips and her smile that drew an aura of light around her face. In the heavy, heady smell of a warm Indian Ocean, I flashed back to Nur's head perched on my chest at the Lho-Nga Mountain lookout. The coconut scent of her hair cocktailing with the slowly decomposing life of the jungle around us. It was also at that lookout, in the light of the disappearing sun and a backdrop of colossal nimbus clouds, that Nur and I first kissed. While the faint rumble moved across a mirror-calm sea and while heavy raindrops fell in slow motion, our lips touched. In the light of the disappearing suns, orange-coloured whirlpools spun in Nur's charcoal eyes, the doors to her soul, allowing me to touch her heart. That of an angel.

I sat cross-legged and waited. I'd almost had enough of the endless breaking of waves and the burning sandflies when I heard her calling. I didn't think of crocodiles or deadly jellyfish and jumped in. Years prior, I'd almost killed myself doing the same thing in the icy waters of Denmark. I thought I'd never see Nur again, but there she was, a glowing apparition. She came to me. We floated only inches apart. Then Nur gazed right through me before her light vanished, before she went inside of me. I surfaced with a gasp and ran back to shore.

'Kenapa! Why?' I cried out.

'Jadi kamu bisa hidup. So you can live.'

And then Nur went silent. Nur had been a living spirit in my life. When I wanted to see her, I would visit the sea. Each time I yearned to die, yearned to be with her. It took me years to do what she had asked of me, not to return to the sea. Nur showed me that the rapture of life is found in love. Nur had lost her entire family at the age of fifteen. She had come home and found them naked in a pile of blood and intestines with chickens fighting over the best pieces. Soldiers had stripped them naked and executed them at gunpoint. They were then gutted. Nur told me she was a freedom fighter with GAM and that her family, the one I had lived with for months on end, was not her own. Nur taught me that love is metaphysical, that it is a gift from God brought to us by angels. She taught me that true love is only felt with courage, when we tell our story with a whole heart. Nur told me everything. The day I left Indonesia, the day I drove past the posters of my own death, and the last time I saw Nur, her voice and words rang repeatedly in my mind: 'Lose what you are afraid of losing, so you stop being afraid.'

Nur was my guardian soul, that woman who allowed me to understand that with love comes faith, not belief. To lose what we cherish the most is to lose our fear, and thus we are free to love. Nur made me the man I am today. Without knowing, I would over the years go back to that night. I still do, and each time I move beyond who I thought I was. Alone but never frightened in those moments where I surrender to her voice which lives inside of me.

It didn't take long before I left Australia. The marred minds of prejudice brought me to the end of my tether. Tanami did not understand and I forgave her. She had grown up in Western Australia, in Guildford, a predominantly White suburb with white picket fences and the pretending that everything was just fine. I thought that was the end of my Australian adventure, but the truth was my journey had just begun. Tanami came across the world and brought with her the life lessons fate had in store for me. They were the ones we have to sleep in the rain to understand, those which tell us what life is truly about. Four days after Tanami became pregnant, she left Denmark and went back to Australia. Suddenly the island at the bottom of the dusty globe in our childhood would take on a new meaning. When Zaki was born, I tried reasoning with Tanami, but it was pointless.

'When can I see Zaki?'

'When I say so.'

I felt as if she had pierced me with a sword, twisting the blade and pulling me closer, stretching her lips in a raging smile. I was confused, heartbroken and a castaway. I spent the first three years in Australia in and out of the family court. Bit by bit I was given the time to be a father to my son. I kept to court appearances after lunch, which somehow worked in my favour. It kept my heart free from hatred, free of grudges and kept my son close to my heart. My world changed once again. The prejudice I'd experienced in Denmark, which had led me down dark roads in my youth but on to rewarding life experiences as I grew older, resurfaced. After all, my name was Mohammed, and I quickly learned that in Australia that was a huge obstacle. Not only in the courtroom where I had to defend allegations of possible child abduction, but also in everyday life. *Mohammed* was not an asset in New Holland. The climb was steep, much steeper than I'd thought, but I kept climbing.

I kept my overseas assignments as a photographer and journalist. In 2014, I was in Gaza for a Danish NGO. At a morgue, I met Omar. Omar had lost almost his entire family in an Israeli bombing raid in 2009. Together with his brother, they opened one fridge door after the other, searching for something about a body they could recognise. The children were piled three or four in a tray. Omar had done the same five years earlier. He told me it had been a moment of quiet grief when he found his beloved and two children covered in blood and dust. Factions had tried to recruit him to fight but he refused and he said words I will never forget. He shed tears that fell into the well of my own soul. The words that I brought with me to my life in Australia were the words that fate wanted me to understand, 'There is only freedom through forgiveness.'

We were in the midst of a war. In the midst of the holy month of Ramadan, which is divided into the spiritual journeys of mercy, forgiveness and freedom from hell. Forgiveness for others is the only way to seek forgiveness for one's self. Reading the Quran, I questioned whether it was really that easy. Could Omar find his spring of forgiveness through those lines: 'You do not do evil to those who do evil to you but you deal with them with forgiveness and kindness'? Could I?

I spent weeks ruminating through sleepless nights. I was haunted by the faces and voices of the war but, more than anything, by Omar's words. I remembered the voices I'd heard in Aceh twelve years before Gaza, when Islamic Sharia law was introduced as official policy overnight, hailed as a symbol of independence and freedom. I remembered how the freedom Nur and I had enjoyed died just as fast. I recalled the cuffs around my wrists, the whispers around me in the dirty prison. 'There will be no freedom. We will do to ourselves exactly what has been done to us.'

But fate kept coming back, this time with the key of forgiveness. Another shot at freedom. One rainy morning, a year after I'd met Omar, Tanami and I kissed again. I needed to climb even higher. Zaki was four years old. I looked calmly at Tanami and asked her what had changed.

'You're different,' she said.

'What's different?'

I didn't feel different. Tanami moved her tongue over her lips and gave me a questioning look. My heart thumped. She turned her glance to my hands and held them in her hands.

They were, as always, the only part of herself she couldn't hide. 'Would you like to kiss again?'

We spent three years together. I was grateful for every single moment, although I never felt that kiss of hers. When she didn't want to let me travel with Zaki alone, we all went together. We went back home and stayed with my family in Suez. It was a cultural shock to Tanami. I'd warned her but I hadn't warned myself. I imagined that her fate had sent her running down her own mountain. My climb got even steeper yet.

Tanami was smart, fierce and independent. I learned a lot from her and about her. At times, I sensed, more than she liked. The lessons applied to myself as well: that nothing we think, say, feel or do has more meaning to it than we give it. It didn't take long before our cultural differences were uncovered again. We tried debating privilege, but how can one debate privilege with someone privileged unless they're prepared to own up to their privilege? Once again, I understood and forgave, but it didn't take long before we discovered that one cannot take on the privilege of another person. Privilege is when something doesn't matter to you because it doesn't matter to you personally. It didn't take long before we found our conversations stalled in choked desolation.

The blessing turned into a blow. As I began writing my first novel, I learned about Australia beyond courtrooms, love and prejudice. My son's grandfather Jim became my editor, and a friendship developed. He was a former journalist and told me about a sordid past. Jim revealed the secrets that are rarely told within or beyond the borders of Australia. He would lock his front door from the inside as if the walls had ears. He'd whisper his stories. 'Our history books are full of lies. We say sorry but the truth is we're bloody well not. We might have stopped killing the Blacks with guns but we're still killing them. They don't tell the kids that Rottnest Island was a concentration camp with corpses still in the ground. Instead, they send them camping there, our own fucking Auschwitz. Mate, you're a second-class citizen in this country and they'll let you know every single day.' Jim had seen the flogging of Aboriginal people, the pouring of salt and vinegar in open wounds and the vigilante executions of the near past. He served me his daughter's court documents throughout my parental ordeal but never passed a judgement. His only words were, 'Love can be a mountain without a peak. Don't fall down trying to reach the top.' My heart raced when he said that. Love can be a cage for the heart but also for the mind. Once we leave the door open, we understand that leaving is not a crime. And we also understand that love repeats itself. That we are attracted to the emotions we recognise, even if those emotions are of prejudice, even when they leave our soul bleeding.

The pieces began coming together. My life in Denmark had sent me running. From the age of seven until the age of fourteen, I'd had racism as a close friend. It was a good day when there were no fights at school with the other kids. Then I'd just get a remark from the teacher, usually something about Arabs. The men beat up the women. Women had no rights. Boys were circumcised and girls had their clits cut off. Or I was not allowed to go to the toilet to the point I'd shit in my pants and the class would laugh at me. My Danish teacher was the worst. She was the local mayor's wife. The things she asked me, that she expected a ten-year-old boy to answer! When we had cooking class, she'd make sure it was pork. I'd cook it but give it to another student to eat. She knew and I was given the task of cleaning up. I cried. I didn't finish my last year of school in Denmark. I piled up all the chairs and tables and set the whole damn class ablaze. I spent my teenage years in Egypt but their lifestyle was beyond tough for the unlearned. Suddenly I didn't belong anywhere. I went back and forth between two countries, trying to work out what to do. I discovered I knew everything about cars, motorcycles, drugs, guns and even passports. That worked well anywhere but it was a dark and shallow road. I knew how to steal a car in less than twenty seconds, source the best hashish and take on the nationality of my choice.

But it would take me years to understand that what I was running away from was the same thing I was going towards. It was what I knew best. Australia was no different. I'd fallen in love with a woman who criticised me, scorned me and told me everything I knew so well. She was beautiful, successful and popular, but one thing she would do more than anything else was punish me for who I was and wasn't. I wasn't only climbing a mountain. I was laying the mountain myself. Inch by inch and stone by stone.

Yet, my life in Indonesia, that chance journey. The love I felt there, not only from others but by myself and to myself and others, made me feel whole. I was never judged, and in that laying down of arms my soul felt at peace. At peace with its heaven and earth. But more than anything, I felt free, as if I had discovered love in the same way I discovered the freedom of surrendering to the mercy and forgiveness of my maker.

Then fate stripped me naked. I will never know why, but it took it all away again. Again, I believed I didn't deserve it. My life went backwards. I became a grieving man, and the remarkable thing was I could see the souls of those who fate had sent down the same road. Years later, it struck me like an epiphany, a rewind of a VHS tape to a mute section, driving past the poster of myself in Aceh. I didn't just die to get out of there. I died so that I wouldn't die the day I died. Fate spoke to me as a child. It pointed repeatedly to the piece of land at the bottom of the globe. It told me what Nur's father, Ahmed, wrote to me on a piece of paper the day I died: *A man who chooses from his heart will be fighting this world. Remember Allah in your life. He will protect your heart and your courage. Safe journey inshAllah. Your friend. Ahmed.*

I came to a country where I lived in close proximity to my neighbours but without any sense of communion. I came to be faced with the company of myself. I wrote lengthy letters to my family, about the isolation of people into their own private little worlds, their racing home to darkened streets and their watching of a virtual reproduction of life on flickering screens behind curtains and security screens. I wrote about a place where people feared the foreigners, feared the world they could not touch or smell or hear beyond the walls of their own home, let alone their border. I wrote to my parents about seeing lives ephemerally materialised as fairy dust. I wrote about my tears and of my longing for family, friendship, kindness, brotherhood and love. I wrote, wondering why I had to fight Tanami who I wished to love.

Then it happened. I was alone, half-naked, and found myself with eyes wide open. It was almost three in the morning that summer night. I got up, went outside, went back in again and was about to go back to bed when I thought I'd heard her. I went back outside again. For a moment I thought I was going crazy. *Nur?* I got dressed and got on the motorbike. I rode down the highway, past roadworks and road trains, past the city and past the burbs until I saw the dark expanse of the Indian Ocean. I felt as if I was about to have a panic attack. My heart pounded as I waded through the sand, all the way to the edge of the water. I sat down and waited until I could wait no more.

I dropped to my back with the feeling of déjà vu and cried. I sobbed like a boy who couldn't find his mother, my lips shaking, ending each breath in a frightening stutter. Tears blurred my eyes, overflowing across my temples and into my ears. There was no voice, no Nur. I closed my eyes to only darkness. I opened them and there was but the twinkling of stars, the twilight rising. All I could hear were calm waves breaking onto the shore. I was on the edge of a land which had been calling since childhood, but I wanted nothing more than to run away. I was only steps away from taking myself to the worlds I imagined behind my closed eyes.

You wouldn't have known had you seen me on that beach. You wouldn't have known that I was dying. I couldn't have imagined it myself. That I would die on an Australian beach without posters or the epiphany of knowing why I was dying – on this spat of land I'd first seen on the bottom of a dusty globe.

That night *I* was my past self and *I* had finally passed away.

I'd carried the last piece of the puzzle all along. Fate pushed and pulled that night as my universe caved in on itself. I had ignored the indelible marks that the soul-shattering prejudice and hatred had carved through me. I had seen and heard and perhaps even touched how freedom and forgiveness were born out of love, inexplicably the only truth to my conscious existence. Souls and bodies had surrendered. Nur had set us free. Tanami would never. The calling to Australia had begun before I even knew what Australia would mean to me. It was the beginning of a journey that lay at the base of that mountain I was climbing. It was never a real mountain; it was the trajectory of my life. Without fate, I would never have known about it, would not have lived for I would not have suffered.

In the last shade of that night, the stars came down. They fell on me like daggers and I gasped. Before I closed my eyes, there was peace. For a while I only existed in a void of time and space. I felt no pain. I was nothing. Then the world came back. Voices. Laughter. Waves. The sky was blue. Bright. I slowly opened my eyes. I was still stretched out on my back. My jacket was still open. I lifted my head up. There was my helmet. There was the beach. So many people. Clearly, they didn't care about whether I was dead or alive. I dropped my head back down. Closed my eyes and felt a shade cover my face. I opened them to a baby boy arched over me. He waved a green plastic shovel and smiled. His eyes. He had my eyes. It was Zaki. It was me. It was all of us.

THE INNOCENCE PROJECT

Sisonke Msimang

I am a Black South African woman, a writer, a mother, an immigrant. I moved to Australia seven years ago and settled on Noongar land. I came without the permission of Noongar people; I had no idea it was their territory on which I was seeking to live. Instead, I sought and was granted the authorisation of the Commonwealth Government. My passport was stamped and I began to live my life here. Like many migrants, I was aware that Europeans had colonised this land and had brutalised the people they found living here. I knew of the White Australia policy and understood that racism continued to shape the present. However, it is one thing to understand the broad strokes of history and quite another to know the details. When I landed in Perth at the airport, I did not know the specifics. I did not know, for example, that in 1834 seventy Noongar people were killed in Pinjarra by a party of White men led by two of Western Australia's most celebrated leaders, Governor James Stirling and John Septimus Roe. Due to the hard work of Theo and Gloria Kearing, leaders in the Noongar community who refused to allow the forgetting, the Heritage Council of

Australia recognises the site, and many Noongar people commemorate the 28th of October as Back to Pinjarra Day.

I had been living in Perth for five years before I learned of the Pinjarra massacre. I had driven countless times on Stirling Highway and across Roe Street. I had spoken their names over and over without allowing myself to be haunted by their deeds. I felt an enormous sadness. A massacre is not only a cause for outrage, it is certainly that, but it is also a source of pain and deep sadness. Roe and Stirling are celebrated everywhere in the state. Their names are carved into bridges and etched onto roadsides and this serves the awful purpose of obscuring from view their crimes and sins. Their stories of murder and bloodshed hide in plain sight. You can find them if you go looking, but why would you look for answers when it would be so much easier not to ask questions? Ignorance is bliss; a sweet form of innocence that only those privileged enough to have escaped the clutches of history can afford.

The question of how we live with history, how we come to terms with it and reckon with it, and then what we do with its enduring effects on the now and the future, has defined my adult life. Moving to Australia and then realising that I am living on Noongar boodjar has been perhaps the most difficult chapter of my life because it has challenged my own understanding of how you live with the afterlives of colonisation when you were not yourself a colonial subject in that place. In my own country, where my connections to land and language need no explaining, I am relatively innocent. Black South Africans were brutalised and colonised and then subjected to five decades of further segregation even as many other colonisers retreated. As independence movements swept across Africa and Asia, apartheid was hardening. I understand then, how it feels to be colonised. But I was not colonised here, nor was the crime of genocide enacted against Zulu people in the way it was in Western Australia. We had our own troubles with apartheid but they were not the same troubles. So when I arrived here and settled, when I bought a house and enrolled my children in a school named after an Italian town, I became part of a colonial project whose logic has historically been propelled by an interest in eliminating Aboriginal people from this continent. How do I live with this while fighting against it?

The notion of terra nullius was a lie of course, but it was also a sort of fantasy, a wish that spoke to how much easier it would be to colonise an empty land. The desire for Australia to be empty of Aboriginal people, and for it to be a place for Europeans and their descendants, has defined its national personality. The special revulsion reserved for Aboriginal people by many non-Indigenous people is a function of racism of course. It is also a testament to a deep-seated desire to shake off history. The continued existence of Aboriginal people reminds Australians (everyone who is non-Indigenous) that the current political and social arrangements are a function of violence. Aboriginal people remind everyone else that the theft of this land was not a victimless crime. And of course, everyone wants to be innocent.

The need for White (and other non-Indigenous) Australians to be innocent drives how we interact with this continent's history. There are two ways to be innocent. One is to plead ignorance and the other is to justify your actions. Europeans justified colonial theft by arguing that the land was empty as a way of making themselves innocent. There are enough contemporaneous accounts of Indigenous occupation by colonisers themselves to have discredited that lie, but its persistence is important. It provides a sort of ambient cover, casting enough doubt to allow those who wish to be innocent room for manoeuvre. Yet this nation derives its respect and authority from the idea that it is a place where anyone can come and make a success of themselves. Australians see themselves as fundamentally honest, salt-of-the-earth types, who believe in decency and fairness. The myths extolling these virtues are everywhere. Talking about the greatness of the nation is another way of remaking it as innocent of course. Even if it has emerged that the land was stolen and some Aboriginal people were killed in the process, it was for 'a greater good'. Indeed, once they were colonised, Aboriginal people were 'better off'. Colonisation had a civilising intent; it was not simply an economic endeavour but a moral and cultural one. The consistent othering, dehumanisation and denigration of Aboriginal people are part of an ongoing attempt to make them responsible for the treatment they have received since settlement. Because whiteness is always constructed in relation and contrast to blackness, Black people are existentially guilty, stained from the start.

These strategies of deceit and justification are in use everywhere today. Addressing them is a matter of conscience and I have been raised to believe that conscience matters. More importantly of course (and interconnectedly), addressing the lies and justifications that underpin the story of Australia is a matter of justice and for many of us, not least of all Aboriginal people living in the country now known as Australia, it is a matter of life and death.

One way of addressing them is to recognise them and to make them explicit when we see them. The project of aggrandising Australia relies on diminishing Aboriginal people. It always has and it continues to do so today. In recent times, that project has taken the form of Bill Leak cartoons admonishing Aboriginal fathers for imagined delinquency and Peta Credlin rants like the one in which she claimed an Aboriginal mother 'was so high on drugs, [she] put the baby down beside a campfire and the dogs ate half its face off'. Railing against Aboriginal people is a way of affirming whiteness, of upholding the founding principles of civilising Aboriginal people. Indeed, it is no accident that the enduring myth that defines non-Indigenous Australia's relationship with Aboriginal people relates to their supposed inability to care for their children. This takes on a special kind of cruelty, given the history of the Stolen Generation. Yet, it must be seen not simply as cruel, but as part of the ongoing project of inventing White innocence. One of the most profound silences that exists in Australia relates to the White people who stole those generations.

In the spring of my seventh year of living here, on Noongar boodjar, I encounter a story about a White family that 'adopted' an Aboriginal girl in the 1960s. I stumble upon it, of course. The sorts of stories that involve White guilt rarely present themselves as fully-fledged tales. Like so many other stories about Australia, it was a tale of sorrow and torment dressed up as a story of generosity, and like so much of this nation's history, it was hidden in plain sight, told to me by a neighbour on an ordinary day in suburban Australia.

Picture this: I am at Stuart's house on a Thursday evening

with my partner and my son. Stuart is a friend. He is middle class and has two boys who attend the same primary school as my children. He and his partner have invited us over for dinner. The kids quickly eat with us and then retreat to the games room to keep killing people on screen. After dinner, the four adults sit at the table and talk. We begin by discussing the use of Noongar words in the classroom setting. We are all progressive. We murmur our approval. Stuart's partner, Peter, who grew up in country Western Australia, says this never would have been possible in his school days. Things are changing, we agree agreeably. I tell them a story about how affected my son was by three elders who came to speak to his class about being members of the Stolen Generation. Stuart responds by saying that he has an aunty who is a member of the Stolen Generation. I'm stunned.

'What do you mean?' I ask. He tells me her name is Harriet and when she was six years old, she moved in with his grandmother and became her fifth daughter. He was in university when he first heard of the Stolen Generation, and so he asked his mum, 'Is Aunty Harriet a member of the Stolen Generation? How did she come to live with us?' His grandmother got angry and his mother got defensive and so he didn't push too hard. We talk about it a while longer and I ask lots of questions. I realise this is not a story I have encountered before. I have heard the stories of Aboriginal people whose lives were upended by policies that took them from their parents and communities. I have never heard a White person admit to having taken any of those children. I have heard institutional responses and apologies and excuses and explanations but I have yet to encounter a public narrative in which those who took (in) Aboriginal children speak to that experience.

In the coming days, I am gripped by Stuart's words. I can't stop thinking about Harriet and his family and what it all means. I reach out and ask if I can interview him. He agrees and we sit on my porch, talking in the late-afternoon sunlight. Stuart tells me Harriet was adopted by his grandmother when she was only six, long before Stuart was born. He is not clear on what happened to her parents or how it was exactly that she came to live with them. Apparently, she had been living with another White family in their small farming community in Victoria in the Gippsland area. They had been Methodist, which meant they didn't dance or drink. But then they died, or one of them died; Stuart is not sure whether it was both foster parents or just one. Either way, it meant Harriet had nowhere to go. Stuart's grandmother took in the child. She had four girls. Her older girls, including Stuart's mother, had already left the house. She thought it would be nice to have another one in the mix. Her youngest daughter had just turned twelve and they would be fine together. Harriet was only supposed to stay for a short while apparently, but that short while turned into a longer while and a few years passed. At some point Harriet was asked what she wanted to do; did she want to stay? Stuart is not clear on who asked her this, by which authorities or by which process. By this time Harriet was calling Stuart's grandmother 'Mum' and she said she was happy where she was.

By the time Stuart was born in 1973, Harriet was already an established member of the family. She was the baby, the youngest of his mum's four sisters and the only one who was Black. Harriet was dark-skinned so there was no question about whether she was Aboriginal or not. She didn't blend in the way she might have if she was fairer-skinned. He tells me Harriet was about the same dark-brown skin tone as me. No one said a word about her skin colour or her features and her hair, they just acted like it was normal for a Black person to be plonked into a White family. I ask him why he thinks no one talked about it. He thinks a bit longer and then tells me that his younger sister once asked about it when she was very young but no one really gave her an answer. Stuart's mum and dad moved to Torquay when he was in primary school and so he grew up there with frequent visits to the family farm in Gippsland. Harriet would sometimes come and visit her big sister in Torquay. Stuart remembers that his primary school friends who met her would ask, 'Why is your aunty Black?' Stuart never knew what to say so he would evade the questions or say, 'She just is.' He never asked his mum or his grandmother or told them about the questions.

One time, Stuart recalls, Harriet was sunbathing by the pool. She told him that if she fell asleep, he should wake her up so she didn't get burned. He was still little and he remembers being curious about what her skin would look like if it burned. So, he didn't wake her. When she finally woke up on her own, she was sunburnt and angry. He must have apologised but he was tuned in enough to know that he could not tell her why he'd done it. He knew he wasn't allowed to talk about her skin colour; it was taboo. I push him. I tell him that I find it strange that he didn't ask. He says that, looking back now, 'I guess you didn't ask in case you found out something you didn't want to know.' Aside from Harriet, Stuart does not recall seeing any other Black people when he was growing up. He thinks for a while and then tells me about a trip he took to Uluru when he was a teenager. He remembers seeing a few Aboriginal people, 'But they acted like us, so they didn't really leave an impression. They were tour guides.'

When Stuart was fourteen, Harriet got married to a guy named Terry. He was an Aboriginal man and he did not act like anyone else Stuart had ever met. He was noticeably different from everyone Stuart knew. Of course, Stuart only knew other White people, so it was not hard for him to experience anyone who wasn't White as different. Terry was nothing like the tour guides with whom Stuart had interacted on the family trip to Uluru. Stuart remembers Terry and Harriet's wedding. Hers was also the first wedding he'd ever attended from start to finish – before that he'd been too young to be included. I tell Stuart I find it interesting that Harriet married an Aboriginal man when she had grown up in a White community. I ask if he knows where they met. He has no idea. I ask whether they met at school. He doubts it. I ask where Harriet went to school and remind him that Australian schools were segregated in the 1950s and 1960s. The implications of this dawn on him. Stuart's grandmother was a schoolteacher and he can't imagine that she would have let her own child go to a different school from her other children based solely on the colour of her skin. We talk this through for a while agreeing that either way, Harriet's experience would have been lonely. If she did attend school with White children and with her older sibling, she would have been an exception. If she didn't, if she went to a segregated school for Black children, well that speaks volumes. Stuart offers to call his mum to find out so that I can have an answer. I tell him not to. I want to tell this story as it is, which is to say, I want to reflect on what Stuart knows and what he doesn't know. Perhaps to examine what he is afraid to know about his family. Secretly, I want him to call his mum without any further prompting from me. I want the answers to matter to him independently of my probing. He doesn't call her and we keep chatting.

Stuart remembers his mum and grandmother and his aunties being pretty upset at Harriet for marrying Terry. He took her off to Ballarat but then he couldn't find a job. Their marriage didn't go well. He was unemployed for long stretches and his aunties, Harriet's White sisters, often complained saying Terry was lazy. Stuart sees now how loaded that word is. He can also recognise that Terry's problems with unemployment were structural. That Terry and Harriet's lives were shaped by forces bigger than what he could see, bigger than what his gran and his aunties could see. Stuart says his family often referred to Terry's long absences as times when he'd gone 'walkabout' and couldn't be found. But of course, they had no idea what that phrase meant. Even though she had qualified as a nurse, Harriet stopped working. Stuart thinks it is because her pay check was swallowed up by Terry's family's needs. I can't be sure Stuart's assessment is based on anything but family lore.

At eighteen, Stuart went to RMIT to study engineering. In his second or third year, he took a class called Koori Curriculum. Koori Curriculum was about Aboriginal histories and cultures. Stuart took the class for the same reasons as everyone else: he needed the credits. Harriet wasn't on his mind when he signed up. One day in class, the lecturer talked about the Stolen Generations. Stuart had no idea that for decades the Australian Government had facilitated a scheme designed to take Aboriginal children from their families without consent. The lecturer spelled it out factually: over successive generations a scheme had been established, funded and encouraged by government and missionaries with the goal of 'breeding out' Indigenous people and killing their cultures. The kidnappings had taken place under the guise of saving Aboriginal children from delinquent parents and dysfunctional families but of course the individual circumstances of Aboriginal families was a moot point. The system was designed to disperse and destroy Aboriginal people and their cultures, so they no longer presented a problem and a nuisance to White Australians. Stuart was shocked. He immediately thought of Harriet. 'My first thought was, *Oh my goodness that must be how Aunt Harriet came to us!* And then I thought, *Oh God, that's terrible. No, it's too terrible. That can't be how she came to us.*' After class, Stuart called his mum and asked her if Harriet had been part of the Stolen Generation. Since she was so much older than Harriet, Stuart thought she would have a good handle on the details. But she didn't. His mum had no real explanation as to how Harriet became her little sister. Still, she was certain that she was not stolen or brought to them under a veil of deceit. His mother reminded him that taking in Harriet was the Christian thing to do and she got defensive.

We come to the end of Stuart's story. It's as far as either of us is prepared to go. I don't want to pry any further and Stuart doesn't volunteer. Still, what I've heard is a story that provides many clues as to how Harriet came to be living in that house. The story began almost as soon as Europeans decided to colonise this continent but for a long time it was a hidden story. Or perhaps a more apt description is that it was an open secret available to any White person who asked questions, and well known amongst Aboriginal people.

For years Aboriginal and Torres Strait Islander people carried out advocacy, demanding the secrecy end and insisting justice be done. Finally, in 1995, Australia's then attorney-general, Michael Lavarch, established a National Inquiry into the Separation of Aboriginal and Torres Strait Islander Children From Their Families. The terms of reference included a mandate to 'trace the past laws, practices and policies which resulted in the separation of Aboriginal and Torres Strait Islander children from their families by compulsion, duress or undue influence and the effects of those laws, practices and policies'.

Around the same time (just two months later), the South African parliament passed the *Promotion of National Unity and Reconciliation Act* of 1995, which established South Africa's much heralded Truth and Reconciliation Commission (TRC). The mandate of the Commission was to investigate gross human rights violations that were perpetrated during the period of the apartheid regime from 1960 to 1994, including abduction, murder and torture.

The National Inquiry was spoken about in exploratory terms, in an open-ended manner, as though it might find that the separation of Aboriginal kids from their communities wasn't always bad. The TRC on the other hand accepted as a matter of fact that human rights violations had taken place. The Commission saw its role as figuring out what to do about the crimes, whereas in Australia, the National Inquiry would determine what had happened with a view to reshaping future policy. The difference in tone and approach could not have been more different. In South Africa, once the commission was over, the argument was over whether or not White perpetrators would be jailed, whereas in Australia, the debate around the *Bringing Them Home Report* was about whether the state had done anything warranting an apology.

And yet the contents of both reports, the TRC and the National Inquiry, are overwhelming in the way they catalogue the devastation caused by racist state policies in their respective countries. For example, the National Inquiry found that:

> The policy of forcibly removing Indigenous children fell within the international legal definition of genocide. The inquiry noted that from 1948 onwards, the date of the Convention on the Prevention and Punishment of the Crime of Genocide, there were clear statements on the content of the crime of genocide and its unlawfulness. The Commonwealth of Australia ratified the Convention in 1949 and it entered into force in 1951.

The TRC final report was thousands of pages long and its findings were numerous in respect of individual cases, ranging from the high-profile murders of activists like Ruth First and Steve Biko to the thousands of 'anonymous' and mainly Black South Africans who were disappeared, tortured and abused by the death squads of apartheid. Both processes involved public hearings that powerfully captured the experiences of victims and survivors. Yet they were not perfect mechanisms and their outcomes spoke volumes about the political and social constraints in which they operated. In South Africa, the TRC was used as a mechanism for social cohesion and so while it was an important space for Black people, it was also seen as a testing ground for a social experiment that at its heart was about forgiveness and reconciliation. In other words, the TRC was not a neutral space in which victims and their families could express rage and seek justice from those who had wronged them under apartheid. It was a space where truth-telling was mobilised in service of forgiveness, in part because of the power of White supremacy. The country's new leaders understood that the world was watching them with keen interest. They understood there were risks associated with punishing Whites for their involvement in apartheid. The markets had a vested interest in making ordinary White South Africans comfortable. Had White people left South Africa en masse, as many of them threatened to do, the immediate economic consequences would have been significant.

This does not diminish the achievements the TRC was able to make. In an essay marking the twenty-year anniversary of the Commission, Dr Pumla Gobodo points out, 'The TRC laid bare the savagery of apartheid. No longer would it be possible to deny the barbarism of the apartheid state and the men and women who were its executioners.' The TRC sought to put an end to the excuses of those who said they didn't know what was happening under their noses and in their backyards and in the segregated schools their children attended. Still, for those who wanted reparations and accountability, the TRC fell far short of expectations. While the stories of pain and grief were telegraphed across the country through the public hearing process, in the end, the TRC only sent one man, Eugene de Cock, to jail for crimes committed under apartheid. For many Black South Africans this remains a sore spot and a cause for simmering resentment. The TRC delivered truth but it skimped on justice.

In Australia, the National Inquiry grappled with similar challenges. There were some important differences however. In the first instance, the Inquiry was only made possible because of the advocacy efforts of Indigenous rights groups that had worked for years and conducted their own hearings and collected hundreds of stories. The TRC had wide-ranging investigative powers and included the power to refer human rights violations to the courts for prosecutions as well as the power to grant amnesty to perpetrators who were deemed to have expressed sufficient contrition. The Inquiry's work was limited to examining the effects of child removals on Aboriginal children and their families. Still, the Inquiry served as a powerful tool for Indigenous activists. Like the TRC, it provided an opportunity for a holistic story to be told about the damage that had been done to Black people at the hands of the Commonwealth and State Governments. While the grand arc of the story of the Stolen Generations is well known, it bears repeating here because the truth must continue to animate our imaginings for another Australia.

Beginning in the mid-1800s through to the 1970s, the Australian Government, supported by White citizens, removed Aboriginal children from their homes by force in a wide-scale kidnapping operation that has had lasting effects on the social fabric of Indigenous communities across the country. Aboriginal children were stolen from their parents through writ of law. The *Victorian Aboriginal Protection Act* of 1869 was the first law in the country to authorise the removal of Aboriginal children from their parents. In 1905, Western Australia passed the *Aborigines Act*, which removed the legal guardianship of Aboriginal parents and made all Aboriginal children essentially legal wards of the state – allowing the government to take any Aboriginal child from their parents without permission. Children were tricked and lured into leaving their parents. They were offered sweets and told they were going on holidays when in fact they were being snatched and taken away forever.

From the beginning of European settlement, Indigenous children were subject to a keen and terrible interest from White settlers. As the Inquiry report deemed, children were 'kidnapped and exploited for their labour'. Reynolds has noted, 'The greatest advantage of young Aboriginal servants was that they came cheap and were never paid beyond the provision of variable quantities of food and clothing. As a result, any

European on or near the frontier, quite regardless of their own circumstances, could acquire and maintain a personal servant.' As settlement formalised and the state developed, missionaries and government agents saw Aboriginal children as soft targets who would be easy to inculcate with European values. Again, a primary colonial interest from the beginning of settlement was that these children would be easily trained as domestic servants and in other areas of menial labour to advance the colonial project. In addition to an interest in Aboriginal children, colonists took a sharp interest in using Aboriginal people as workers and/or removing them from land earmarked for agriculture. Increasingly in the press, Aboriginal people began to be referred to as a collective nuisance and were treated as though 'their presence was unsettling and embarrassing to non-Indigenous people'.

The more pathologised Aboriginal communities became, the easier it became to justify state intervention in the lives of Aboriginal children. Ironically then, Aboriginal kids were the victims of initiatives aimed at protecting them from the so-called ills of their communities – ills that had been created by massacres and dispossession that were carried out by the same Europeans who were now seeking to 'protect' them. Rather than end the racist policies they had created, the colonists sought to end Aboriginality itself. The best way to stop Aboriginal people from menacing White society would be to eliminate them using the Darwinian tool of 'breeding' them out. The state set about trying to ensure that fair-skinned Aboriginal children were removed from the care of their Black parents and sent to White families and White communities where it was hoped they would marry White and over time reduce the proportion of 'Aboriginal blood' until it was negligible. Darker-skinned children were sent to individual homes or to residences where they were taught skills related to domestic labour.

No one was more committed to the practice of breaking up Aboriginal families than AO Neville. He believed (without any evidence) that 'full-blooded' Aboriginal people would die because they were incapable of surviving modernity. In his opinion, they were, 'a problem' that would 'eventually solve itself'. He insisted, '… they are not, for the most part, getting enough food, and they are, in fact, being decimated by their own tribal practices.' Neville determined, 'In my opinion, no matter what we do, they will die out.' Neville was hugely influential in determining the policies that enabled the kidnapping of Aboriginal children. He was cold blooded and calculating and the calculus of economics was clear in this thinking. As Neville put it:

> I know of 200 or 300 girls, however, in Western Australia who have gone into domestic service and the majority are

> doing very well. Our policy is to send them out into the white community, and if a girl comes back pregnant our rule is to keep her for two years. The child is then taken away from the mother and sometimes never sees her again. Thus, these children grow up as whites, knowing nothing of their own environment. At the expiration of the period of two years the mother goes back into service so it really does not matter if she has half-a-dozen children.

This is the story as we know it. It is the story that was told to great effect and in painful detail at the Inquiry. One of the key findings of the report was that the crimes carried out against Aboriginal people by Commonwealth and state laws meant that the Australian Government constituted genocide. Despite this, upon receiving the *Bringing Them Home Report*, then Prime Minister John Howard refused to apologise to Aboriginal people about the pain successive governments had caused them. Rather than address the substance of the report, Howard famously stated that he did not 'subscribe to the black armband version of history'. The black-armband version of history to which Howard was alluding is 'a brand of Australian history which its critics argue represents a swing of the pendulum from a position that had been too favourable, too self-congratulatory, to an opposite extreme that is even more unreal and decidedly jaundiced'. The black armbanders are said to 'belittle past achievements, encourage a guilt industry and impede rational thinking on current problems'. In other words, Howard saw the horrific acts documented in the report and dismissed them as mere political correctness. As had been the case in South Africa, some White people met the spectacle of Black grief that was so powerfully displayed during the TRC with indifference. Still, there were many others who were moved and who responded with empathy and grief and guilt, who undertook to apologise personally. National Sorry Day began as a spontaneous outpouring of emotion and as a way of acknowledging the resilience and pain of the Stolen Generations. What Australia's inquiry did not do was impose a regime of reparations or address the question of direct personal accountability. In this way, it mirrored the TRC process that I observed just after South Africa gained independence. The inquiry focussed on truth and emotion, but in the end, the authorities who heard these truths were able to ignore the demands for justice and accountability that emerged from the process.

In both South Africa and Australia, the inquiry and the TRC focussed on Black pain but failed to sufficiently account for White culpability. Both processes rightfully centred victims but neither of them provided for any sort of public reckoning for the perpetrators of crimes against Aboriginal children and their parents and families. The acts of institutions were spoken about, but there was no pressure placed on White people to step forward and talk about their personal roles in stealing children. This means that while many people can attest to the pain of the Stolen Generations, there isn't a single White person who can be said to represent the face of White contrition. No significant White Australian icons exist who embody the journey White people in this country need to take.

This is not surprising. In South Africa too there was no White corollary to Nelson Mandela and no White leader who stood in humility and shame and attempted to atone for their sins. Although the last apartheid president, FW de Klerk, was jointly awarded the Nobel Peace Prize alongside Mandela in 1993, it is widely acknowledged that he didn't deserve the prize because he struggled to repudiate apartheid. Perhaps this was why Stuart's story of his aunty was so surprising. I have heard dozens of stories about the experiences of Stolen Generation survivors and I have watched countless hours of testimony at the Truth Commission. Still, until Stuart told me about Aunt Harriet, I had never witnessed up close a White person's attempts to grapple with the truth of their connection to a racist history. And yet, Stuart was instinctively invested in protecting his own and his family's innocence. At a gut level, the impulse towards not knowing continues to shape White

Australia, as it shapes White South Africa. This is a pity. There will be no progress in dismantling White supremacy until good White people are prepared to shed their desire to be innocent of history. Stuart took a few vital steps, though certainly not enough. In another Australia, White people's admissions of guilt will not be so difficult. More importantly, they will be accompanied by consequences. In another Australia, there will be justice.

WARRAN

Epilogue

Nardi Simpson

gubiyaan gigilaygu
wugawa-dhi gubilaygu
waal gungandu
garrabaldaygu
gubiyaan gigilaygu birralii

walanbaa

baawaagu ngarraldanha muyaan. giirr nguungunda nhama muyaan gagaldanha, garril gagaldanha mayrraaga. bungun-nha ganaay, gulagamali warraylanha. yanawaanha nha muyaangu. gabanbaa nha dhina, garaarr, dhaymaarr, dhiyaan muyaangu. yuluwaanha guyaynga, buunhugalga. winangaylanha nha yurrulgubala dhiyaan.

winangaylanha nha guwiinbaa. wiimalaanha nha maa warranga

dhamaldanha buliirralaya, gii, dhuwi bumaldanha. giidjaa
dhuurraanha bidjali maagu. guwiinbaa gaawaanha. yilaa,
baawaa ngarriylanha dhawunda, warranga. giirr nhama
muyaan bulubalaanha buuyandi. baabilaanha gaali
garaydhalibaa, galumalaanha galumay burrul wagibaa
yurrula
gaay guwaaldanha. baluwa gaalingu gaay dhuurraanha.
winangaylanha gaalingu burrul bina. guwaaldanha gaali waal
ngaaybiyaay, gawubiyaaybala
marangiirr
garaydhalibaa
ganadhaawan.gaan
baawaa muyaan guwaldanha dhuningarraay, Burruguugiirr.
ngadhan.gaa gaalingu gaay
ngarrilaya winangaylaya, yanaaynbilaanha, wuudhanha
muyaan. garrilyaa, dhayaarryaa, warranyaa, ngawiylanhayaa
guyaynyaa. gaba nguungu baawaaga guwaaldanha muyaan
gaay. giirr nhama muyaan guwaaldaya-nginda. yilaa nguungu
wuudhanha burrbiyaan baawaagu.

maagu baawaa ganaay, bundaagilanha maagu muyaan. gayaa
baawaa.

dhirranbalanha nguungu maa
gaagilaanha nguungu citygu buwarr

gundhidja baawaalaa, maa nha gaay gaagilanha. mara
gimbilanha gaay, nguwalanha wirringaaga yurrunda.
gulagamalanha nha. winangaylanha nguungu dhiyaangiirr,
ngurrambaagiirr
waan nha ngarrandi barrgingu.giirr nhama burrulaa yaadha
waan! burranbalanha nha maa yinggil
burranbalanha nha buya bayn. yilaa baarramalanha maa,
galan. garriyanginda baawaa, dhirralanhabala burrbiyaan
muyaangu. mubal, dharra yurringgalanha maa. baawaa
muyaan winangaylaya gawu gimbilanha
guwaalaanha,
gigilanha,
dhurralaanha
dhaarriwaanha bayn, yinggil baawaaga
winangaylanha nha burrbiyaan, maa. dhiirraylanha maa
marangu, gaymalanha, gimbildanha. banagawaanha nha
buurraanda.
guwaymadhan,
mirriyaa

dhinawan dhingaa
dhurralaanha nha, gimbildanha nha,
yilaa gaangaywaanha
dhuningarraay nhuubala, nhalay nhamabala, wirringgaa
muyaanbala,
manday maliyaa mayabuu
gayanhi yulaay
maa dharra
walanbaa bayamalanha
dhugay.

Strong

Sister sees a tree. It calls to her, leaves beckoning in the breeze. Its arms are outstretched waiting to hug. She walks towards it. Her feet are light, the grass and soil the tree's kin. She dances between the clumps and blooms. She knows the bush has family too.

When she is near, she greets and gives thanks. She places her hand on the trunk. Touching, they breathe together, heart and heart wood beating in time. Ants crawl from bark to hand. They connect the two, confirming their bond. Then sister sits on the ground between roots of the tree. It shades her from the heat. They stay this way – without words, still. Caring and cared for in the big plain scrub.

They talk. Their words are slow. Their thoughts wise. They speak not with their mouths but with their minds. Like the ancients. Silent. Deep. Sister and tree talk in old ways. Their language is of thought.

After sitting and thinking together, tree releases and gifts itself. Maybe a leaf, sometimes bark, other times root or fragrance or flower. It is happy sister speaks language of tree. It wants to keep talking so gives of itself. Sister's hands open and the tree falls into them. Sister is grateful. Her hands tingle. She cradles her gift, all the way back into the city.

When sister is home her hands take over the yarn. They make the story, folding words of woman and tree. She caresses tree's gift; treats it like her own family, own country. She works from dusk to dawn. Many days over. Her hands get tired. Her bones start to ache. Fingers blister then peel. Sister thinks about stopping but the tree pushes her body. Belly and legs urge hands on. Mind makes images of sister and tree together– talking, becoming, growing. Sister's pain and tiredness fade. Her body and hands remember. They know the movements of her ancestors' hands, their movement and making and skill. Memory shoots through her veins; guwaymadhan, lignum, emu meat. It flows and she makes, and soon it is born. Old but new, here but there, woman but tree. Generations, friends expanding through lifetimes. Twisted and tied– hand and branch strong, holding, always.

** illustration by baawaa ngay (my younger sister), Lucy Simpson*

AFTERWORD

Lena Nahlous

When I first stepped into the role of CEO at Diversity Arts Australia (DARTS), I had discussions with people invested in championing cultural and racial equity about how to centre artists and art itself through advocacy. We spoke about how to embed artists and their work into a national organisation like DARTS, to support transformative change.

These conversations were the seeds that germinated the Stories from the Future project, a prospective futures project we executed through national workshops to record the aspirations and ambitions of creatives and the current state of play for underrepresented and marginalised artists. Stories from the Future invited First Nations and culturally diverse creatives across Australia to share their visions for a different kind of arts and creative sector. We developed a framework for doing this that would take us outside of every day, outside of the binary positions, the constant responding and talking back to seemingly immovable systems and structures not designed for us. Instead, we invited creatives to set their agendas on their terms. Embedded into this project was the idea of commissioning writers to lead the conversation by creating new work.

As a result, we developed a partnership with Sweatshop Literacy Movement to produce *After Australia*, featuring predominantly speculative fiction, which was published in 2020 at the onset of the pandemic. Additionally, the book went to press during severe natural disasters like the January 2020 bushfires. In a time of conflict and uncertainty, *After Australia* dared to imagine radical and intersectional futures, while engaging with Australia's fraught past.

Following the success of *After Australia*, we planned the second book in the series—this time, a collection rooted firmly in the present. *Another Australia* traverses history, untold stories and erasure, and offers narratives of another Australia than is usually portrayed. *Another Australia* brings together some of Australia's most compelling established and emerging contemporary writers. Their mix of personal stories, essays, fiction and poetry reflects these uncertain times and touches on unexplored themes of a pandemic, domestic abuse, climate change, racism, family, community and erased histories. The pages in this volume do heavy lifting, dissecting and exploring language, exile, war, diaspora, migrant complicity in colonisation, and living on stolen land. These stories give voice to the bleak and confrontational issues that have become part of our everyday reality, issues that are often silenced to sustain a narrow narrative of what Australia is. These stories are also affirming, uplifting, and threaded with humour and resilience. The artists boldly raise questions, embrace vulnerability and provide perspectives that concern us all.

Thank you to the writers of *Another Australia*. Congratulations to Sweatshop and Affirm Press for their work on *Another Australia*, particularly to the anthology's editor and Sweatshop General Manager Winnie Dunn for her dedication and skill in curating this powerful and reflexive collection of writing. Thank you also to Sweatshop Founding Director and author Dr Michael Mohammed Ahmad for his critical work in platforming culturally diverse and First Nations writers. Thank you to the team at Affirm Press, notably Martin Hughes and Ruby Ashby-Orr, for supporting these critical stories and giving them a national audience. Gratitude to our dedicated team at Diversity Arts, notably Glaiza Perez, associate producer of Stories from the Future, the project of which this book is a component. Thank you to our Stories from the Future partners across the country, particularly to Dr Remy Low at the University of Sydney.

Supporting this work is foundational to both Diversity Arts and my purpose. To play a corroborative role is significant. As a Lebanese girl growing up in Western Sydney, I rarely saw my community represented in books, TV or the media outside of nightly news stories about civil war, crime and terrorism. This distorted my sense of self, and I've dedicated my professional career to helping change these narratives. So, what is the value of an anthology like *Another Australia?* It provides readers encouragement and nourishment; it disrupts and counters the narratives that seek to erase histories and stories of Australia; it acts as a source of empowerment, serving as proof, bearing witness and providing a space for people to navigate thorny terrain.

IT TAKES A VILLAGE TO REWRITE THE NATION ...

THE TEAM

Editorial Advisor: Michael Mohammed Ahmad

Cover Artist: Josh Durham, Design by Committee

Design and Typesetting: Mike Kuszla

Publication Publicist: Laura McNicol Smith

Publishing Director, Affirm Press: Martin Hughes

Senior Editor, Affirm Press: Ruby Ashby-Orr

Executive Director, Diversity Arts Australia: Lena Nahlous

Associate Producer, Diversity Arts Australia: Glaiza Perez

THE EDITOR

Winnie Dunn is the General Manager of Sweatshop Literacy Movement and the editor of several critically acclaimed anthologies, including *Sweatshop Women.* She is a writer of Tongan descent from Mount Druitt and holds a Bachelor of Arts from Western Sydney University. Her work has been published in *The Guardian, HuffPost, Griffith Review, Meanjin* and *SBS Voices.* Winnie is currently completing her debut novel, *Dirt Poor Islanders*, which will be published by Hachette in 2023.

THE WRITERS

SHANKARI CHANDRAN is a Tamil–Australian lawyer who was raised on Ngunnawal Country and now lives and raises her four children on Darug Country. She is the author of three books: *Song of the Sun God* (Perera-Hussein Publishing, 2017), *The Barrier* (Pan Macmillan Australia, 2017) and *Chai Time at Cinnamon Gardens* (Ultimo Press, 2022). Her work was longlisted for the International Dublin Literary Award (2019), and shortlisted for the Fairway National Literary Award (2018) and the Norma K Hemming Award for Speculative Fiction (2018). She is the recipient of the Blake-Beckett Trust Scholarship (2019), the Create NSW Writers' Fellowship (2018/2019) and grants from the Australia Council for the Arts (2021) and Create NSW (2022). Shankari is the Deputy Chair of Writing NSW.

OSMAN FARUQI is an award-winning journalist, editor and author. He is regularly published in *The Sydney Morning Herald*, *The Age*, *The Guardian* and *The Monthly*. He holds adjunct roles at the University of Sydney and the University of New South Wales. His debut book on race in Australia is due for release in 2022.

DECLAN FRY is a writer, poet and essayist. Born on Wongatha country in Kalgoorlie, he has been awarded a Peter Blazey Fellowship, the Lord Mayor's Creative Writing Award for memoir, and was shortlisted for the Judith Wright Poetry Prize. He currently lives with his partner, their pup Walnut, and a cat, Turnip. @_declanfry.

AMANI HAYDAR is an award-winning writer, visual artist, lawyer and advocate for women's health and safety based in Western Sydney. Amani's debut memoir *The Mother Wound* was awarded the 2022 Victorian Premier's Literary Award for Non-fiction. Amani is a former Archibald Prize finalist and has had both her writing and art featured in several publications including *Racism*, *Arab Australian Other*, *Sweatshop Women Volume Two*, SBS Voices and ABC News Online.

SHIRLEY LE is a Vietnamese–Australian writer from Western Sydney. She is a Creative Producer at Sweatshop Literacy Movement and holds a Bachelor of Arts from Macquarie University. Her short stories and essays have been published in *Overland*, *The Guardian*, *SBS Voices*, *The Griffith Review*, *Meanjin* and several Sweatshop anthologies. Shirley is currently working on her debut novel as the recipient of a 2019 Affirm Press Mentorship.

L-FRESH THE LION is one of Australia's most important hip-hop artists and was born and raised in South-West Sydney. In the time since his ARIA-nominated album *BECOME* was released (2016), L-FRESH The LION has taken his music to the world. Alongside festival appearances all over Australia, he addressed the United Nations Headquarters in New York in late 2018. He was also selected as an ambassador for YouTube's Creators For Change global initiative, with his resulting video *RACI$T / OUR WORLD* premiering at the Tribeca TV Festival in New York. Breaking ground and exceeding expectations is a recurring theme of this South-West Sydney artist, having performed alongside hip-hop icons such as Nas, Talib Kweli, Dead Prez, and even the legendary Sir Elton John. L-FRESH The LION continues to take things to the next level.

MOHAMMED MASSOUD MORSI is a writer with a talent for reaching to the heart of existence in a complex world. His work is invariably raw and powerful as he looks to important questions, finding that which is quintessentially human within much broader struggles. His work is enriched by his photographer's eye for detail and a passion for speaking out for those suppressed. Morsi's debut novel, *The Palace of Angels* (Wild Dingo Press, 2019) was shortlisted for the 2020 NSW Premier's Literary Awards and the 2020 Voss Literary Prize.

SISONKE MSIMANG is the author of *Always Another Country: A memoir of exile and home* and *The Resurrection of Winnie Mandela: A biography of survival.* She is a South African writer whose work is focused on race, gender and democracy. She has written for a range of international publications including *The New York Times, The Washington Post, The Guardian, Newsweek* and *Al Jazeera.* Sisonke is the curator of the literature and ideas program at Perth Festival.

OMAR MUSA is a Bornean-Australian author, visual artist and poet from Queanbeyan, Australia. He has released four poetry books (including *Killernova*), four hip-hop records. His debut novel *Here Come the Dogs* was long-listed for the International Dublin Literary Award and Miles Franklin Award and he was named one of the Sydney Morning Herald's Young Novelists of the Year in 2015. His one-man play, *Since Ali Died*, won Best Cabaret Show at the Sydney Theatre Awards in 2018. He has had several solo exhibitions of his woodcut prints.

SARA M SALEH is a daughter of migrants from Palestine, Egypt and Lebanon, living and learning on Gadigal land. A long-time human rights campaigner, writer and poet, Sara's essays, poems and short stories have been published in English and Arabic in *The Guardian, SBS, Australian Book Review, Overland, Meanjin, Australian Poetry Journal, Cordite Poetry Review, Sweatshop Women, A Blade of Grass, Making Mirrors, Solid Air* and *Borderless.* Sara is the first Australian poet to win both the *Australian Book Review*'s Peter Porter Poetry Prize (2021) and the *Overland* Judith Wright Poetry Prize (2020). #SayMashAllah. Sara co-curated the anthology *Arab, Australian, Other* (Picador, 2019) and is developing her debut novel, *Songs for the Dead and the Living* (Affirm Press, 2023).

NARDI SIMPSON is a Yuwaalaraay storyteller from NSW's north-west freshwater plains. Her debut novel, *Song of the Crocodile*, was the 2018 winner of the black&write! Fellowship, longlisted in 2021 for the Stella Prize, Australian Book Industry Awards – Literary Fiction Book of the Year, and shortlisted for the Victorian Premiers Literary Awards – Indigenous Writing, MUD Literary Prize, New South Wales Premier's Literary Awards – New Writing, and the Indie Book Awards – Debut Fiction. As a member of Indigenous folk music duo Stiff Gins, Nardi has travelled nationally and internationally for the past twenty-two years, performing in the US, UK, Ireland, Canada, Vietnam and the Pacific Islands, and is currently in her second year of PhD study through ANU School of Music in Composition. Nardi continues to be heavily involved in the teaching and sharing of culture in both her Sydney and Yuwaalaraay communities.

ANNE-MARIE TE WHIU is a Māori-Australian writer, weaver, producer. She is the co-editor of *Whisper Songs* and *Solid Air: Australia and New Zealand Spoken Word*. Her writing has been published in Australia and Aotearoa. Anne-Marie is a recipient of The Wheeler Centre Next Chapter Fellowship 2021.

Another Australia is published by Affirm Press in partnership with Sweatshop Literacy Movement in association with Diversity Arts Australia

Diversity Arts Australia (DARTS) is assisted by the Australian Government through the Australia Council and by the NSW Government through Create NSW

Previously, by Sweatshop and Diversity Arts Australia …

Climate catastrophe, police brutality, white genocide, totalitarian rule and the erasure of black history provide the backdrop for stories of love, courage and hope. In this unflinching new anthology, twelve of Australia's most daring Indigenous writers and writers of colour provide a glimpse of Australia's past, present and future as we head toward the year 2050.

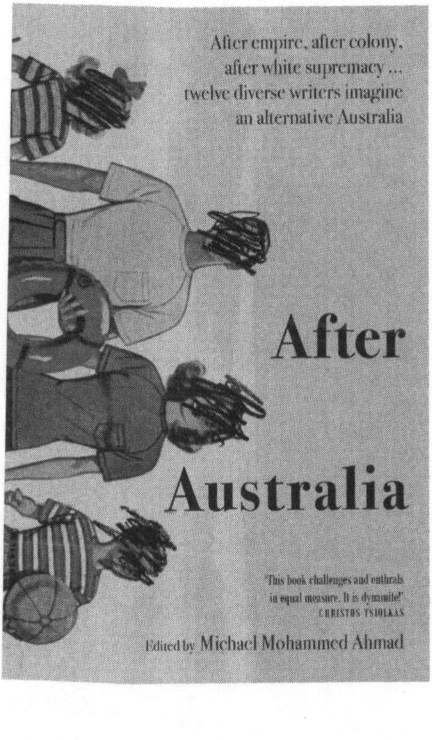

FEATURING

Claire G. Coleman

Hannah Donnelly

Future D. Fidel

Roanna Gonsalves

Ambelin Kwaymullina

Kaya Ortiz

Michelle Law

Zoya Patel

Sarah Ross

Omar Sakr

Khalid Warsame

Karen Wyld